My God Box

My God Box

Parable of the Incorrigible Child

Margaret Iuculano

Penance Publishing

For further information, please contact:
www.margaretlano.com
penancepublishing@hotmail.com

Printed in the United States of America

My God Box
Margaret Iuculano

1. Title 2. Author 3. Memoir/Biography

LCCN: 2007940720

ISBN-10: 0-9801415-0-8
ISBN-13: 978-0-9801415-0-4

This book traveled from conception to print thanks to the unwavering support and inspiration of God, who empowers every thought and action associated with my life. My God Box is a testament to the power of faith and an expression of my gratitude for the Lord's guidance and repeated intervention in my life.

Table of Contents

Acknowledgements

I am grateful to the following people who believed in me and played a part in helping me on my journey to success: Richard Ludden, Ed Phillips, Joe Lahurd, Rich Cocchiaro and Ray Morganti. Thanks also to my loving sister Cindy who has been my backbone and source of strength during the past 5 years. You all exhibited an amazing faith in me even without realizing how much I needed it!

I would also like to express my appreciation to my mother and Uncle George for giving me the life-altering experience of an unforgettable childhood that built and strengthened my character, and encouraged me to become the woman I am today.

Thank you to Nancy Genovese, who without her writing skills this book would not have come to be. Thanks for setting in motion my mission to alleviate suffering and misery in others.

And last but not least, thanks to Joel Hochman at Arbor books for allowing me to discuss my book project for 2 years before getting started.

Most of all very special thanks to my amazing husband, Anthony who always believing in me, has saved me in more ways than he knows and to my wonderful children, Chalice and Anthony who have taught me how to love.

Thank you God for placing all these phenomenal people on my life's path.

A Testament to the Presence of God: The Faith Factor

*"If you have faith like a mustard seed, you
will say to this mountain, 'Remove from here';
and it will remove. And nothing will be
impossible to you."*
—Matthew 17: 19

When I decided I no longer wanted to be unhappy, I knew I could not succeed alone. When I realized I had shed my last tear, I knew it was thanks to my faith in God. Likewise, when I discovered I had stepped out from the cold dark clouds and into the warm light, I was fully aware it was due to the presence of the Lord in my life.

This is my journey; a long meandering expedition filled with obstructed paths, seemingly dead-end cull-de-sacs and an endless series of off-course detours. But hearing the Lord's 'voice' respond to my cry—"where is God," I knew I was moving in the direction of my destination.

The power of faith gave me the happiness I knew I deserved. I was able to retrieve my inner strength, find my dignity and free a life force, shackled in circumstances beyond my control. I soon discovered that living in faith was not only my survival, but my triumph.

Therefore, a firm believer in giving back, and grateful for the blessings I have received, I feel empowered to share my own personal struggles to help others explore and experience the curative, uplifting energy of faith.

Although I have been healed and have no need to ever return to my past, I am retaking this journey to inspire and reassure. With faith, even the most menacing demons can be defeated.

It was from these thoughts and intentions that *My God Box* was conceived. Written neither in tears nor anger, but with serenity and acceptance in my heart, this book is intentioned to enlighten and empower. I set my thoughts, feelings and experiences in print to disclose how a belief in the Divine Force led me to find God in the midst of my own emotional and physical holocaust.

My God Box is not only a testament to the strength of faith, but an announcement of my mission to offer my insights and lessons learned, to help all those who may be suffering the painful and humiliating persecution bred of abuse, exploitation and cruelty, in all its toxic shadings.

Truthfully, I did not discover the power and value of faith overnight. In fact it took me quite some time to develop a spiritual life and a trust in the Lord. My parents were predominately non-believers who took me to church on rare occasions. Contrary to my beliefs, they felt a relationship with God was an adult issue and not essential during the growing up years. Children just didn't need God! Instead, they believed that when the time was right, they would choose a religion and accept baptism as the energy to embrace a spiritual life.

Therefore my journey into the light was filled with hindering road blocks and crippling impediments. For a long time I probed in the darkness, fighting with my doubts and uncertainties, struggling with unanswered questions. Most of the time I just closed myself up, unable to deal with the excruciating agony and loneliness.

Catching my image from time to time in photos, I was frightened by the slouching, grim-faced girl with an aura of hardness far too premature to even begin to understand, let alone accept. I was dreadful to look at— my image was an appalling reflection of my state of mind. Something had to change!

My epiphany occurred during my early teens, when I realized not everyone lived a life tinged with such uncertainty and despondency. Observing the well-adjusted, gratifying lives of others, I became envious of the smiles I didn't smile, and the laughter missing from my heart. Longing for an end to the misery, I questioned—"Why can't I be happy? Why are my eyes dull and clouded with tears? Where was the glow of excitement and delight all the other kids had? Why did some people have so much while I had absolutely nothing?"

The answers did not come and the questioning continued to invade my thoughts, turning my anxieties and frustrations into anger. Uncomfortable with my situation and distressed by who I was becoming, I felt I had absolutely nothing to lose by trying prayer. I found myself trapped in a box with my back against the wall. I had no one to turn to and nowhere to go. But I bowed my head and waited—unaware of what I should say or what if anything I had a right to ask for.

Besides daily prayer to nurture me through my struggles, I developed little catch phrases which eventually became my mantra during trying times. Though certainly not a substitute for prayer, they were an accompaniment and an ally in defeating the often insurmountable challenges I had to face. Then, one day, during a moment of dialogue with God it came to me.

I threw up my arms gazing at the heavens—"I must make a choice," I blurted out, "stay on the path I select no matter what, and always keep the faith." I liked how the words sounded and began to repeat the phrase over and over until it became a constant chant. The words were energizing—but would I be able to honor the commitment?

Being true to myself was in a sense an additional challenge—perhaps even the most difficult. However, once the decision was made I resolved not to falter.

Drifting between jostling doubts and a personal crusade to change, every morning I discussed with myself the day's strategies. I knew that if I wanted to achieve my goals I would not be able to wander off track. Yet the temptation was cajoling, and the intervention of negative forces continued to unsettle my feathers.

The more determined I was to follow my path, the more these sinister influences tried to invade my life. At times it was a tug-of-war—a series of torturous pulls, dragging me between good and evil. Yet I knew that if I didn't do something to transform my life, not only would I be stuck in this abyss of depravity, but it would be my downfall.

Although I was battling something much greater than myself—something over which I had no control, I promised myself I would accept the hand I was dealt, but play it to win the game. How? By summoning God to help me forge ahead, take control and never look back.

Enlightened, I realized I was the protagonist of my own life, not a spectator viewing the scenario from the balcony. And as a participant, I was fully involved in every decision, event and experience. I lived each moment intensely and with the intention to set my mind on moving forward, never daring to take a step back.

Managing my circumstances forced me to live life as an accomplice instead of a sightseer observing from the outside as the days and years spun out of control. However, with the empowerment of faith and the energy siphoned from a belief in God's providence, I was able to grab the reins, redirect my life and inevitably make a difference.

Devising a motto, I kept it throughout my life: "Aerodynamically the bee cannot fly. However, since it does not know this, it flies!"

It was and is a powerful concept—and how inspiring! My faith, on the other hand was a life altering motivator, encouraging me to both create and maintain a positive attitude in the light of a steady stream of adversities. Many times I could have crumbled under the weight of it all. But the hope, faith ignited kept me standing tall and loyal to my commitments to get behind the helm of my life and navigate it to where I wanted it to go.

In the beginning, before my 'encounter' with God, I trudged around hiding behind a dysfunctional label, pitying myself as a victim. It was almost an excuse for my misery. I could not be happy—I was a misfortunate victim. I focused on this regretful lot, not realizing I was achieving exactly what I was believing—I was victimizing myself! And the woe-is-me attitude served only to push me further down. This was certainly not my objective. But what was? It was to move forward into the life I wanted and deserved. If I made mistakes along the way, I learned from them, never repeated them and continued along my path a good deal wiser.

My God Box is the revelation of how I shattered the victim mindset; a self-defamatory attitude that actually made me more of a victim than the devastating circumstances of my life. With the help of God I was able to interrupt the injurious sequence of negativity and concentrate on utilizing my faith to rid me of the fears and insecurities that had kept me in an impasse.

My family genealogy contained a lineage of grandparents, parents and a step-father; a pedigree of abused individuals who matured into abusers. Horrible—yes, but they taught me how not to be. Determined to be different, I learned the lesson. Swimming against the tide, I successfully 'broke the cycle'—and all it took was a mustard seed of faith.

> *"If we pray, we will believe; if we believe we will*
> *love; if we love we will serve."*
> —Mother Teresa

The Book of
Genesis

Chapter 1

In the Beginning

"God created man in his image…
Male and female he created them."
—Genesis 1:27

Sometimes it is challenging to actually recognize, let alone accept the God-like goodness in other human beings. Many times it is difficult to love one another as is written in the Bible and perceive every man, woman and child as one of the Lord's creations.

Often the 'image and likeness' which mankind shares with the Divine becomes obscured by egoism if not willful misdeeds. And for a small child, being reared in an environment of abuse, neglect and rejection, the consequences of a strong dislike and or mistrust of others can be not only life-altering, but prevalent for a lifetime.

Unhappy with my circumstances, I decided the choice was mine to either accept defeat and its penalty or rebel and strive to overcome. Fortunately, I chose survival.

When the Lord said, *"Let the earth bring forth vegetation: seed bearing plants and all kinds of fruit trees that bear fruit containing their seed,"* He was not only designing the universe, but all its inhabitants. We all come from the tiniest of seeds, and we sprout and grow, nurtured by those who have sown the seeds—our parents.

My mother Vivian, a *petite* slender girl with long black hair that glistened in the sunlight and dark, expressive, almond-cut eyes, was proud of her Native American Heritage. The daughter of Vivian Patton, my Irish, Black Dutch grandmother, she also had a branch on the family's genealogical tree not to distant from her grandfather, General Patton.

Statuesque at six feet tall, my grandmother had a head of flaming red hair and a fiery personality to match. Undoubtedly, Vivian Patton was a rather striking woman, unique and pretentious, and certainly not easily forgotten.

However, plagued throughout her life with crippling bouts of depression, my grandmother was dysfunctional and infamous for popping pills and patronizing the couch—all while neglecting and mistreating her children. In a sense as a perpetrator of maltreatment, she nourished the seed of abuse. A multi-generational 'woe,' it spread until finally destroyed.

Vivian Patton was married to Chet Allen, my mother's father. A handsome military man with Cherokee blood running through his veins, he had a pleasing glance and a charismatically engaging disposition. With his warm smile, the charming Chet was a sharp contrast to his eternally sulking wife, who seemed almost frozen in a perennial scowl.

Living on an emotional roller coaster, with an unstable mother who used violence and the withholding of warmth and affection to discipline her children, my mother sought fulfillment of her needs outside the family. Desperately yearning for the love denied, she was immediately captivated by the thrill of her 'first love.' The couple dated and before long the relationship turned serious.

Steve Panks, the first generation American son of affluent German immigrants was a blue-eyed, sandy-haired fellow who at eighteen years of age was just two years older than my mother. His attentions and alluring personality were a new and exciting experience. Consequently, the teen-aged girl basked in the elated feeling of being at the center of someone's attentions. It was a different sensation and a welcome swing from her life of deprivation and abandon.

Handsome, persuasive and adept at the art of seduction despite his young age, it didn't take long for Steve to infatuate my mother and gain her active attentions. Soon after she discovered she was 'in a family way.' Terrified by the overbearing circumstances my mother confessed to her estranged parents.

In 1966, out of wedlock babies were labeled illegitimate, and likewise scorned along with the women who gave them life. Therefore, although Chet and Vivian were divorced and living separate lives, when they learned of their daughter's shameful predicament they agreed on the plan of action that needed to be taken. Once informed, Steve's parents were in full agreement.

Without hesitation both sets of parents made their wishes known to the young couple. There was just one remedy—marriage. And without protest or discussion, Steve and my mother said their 'I dos' several months before I was born on September 30, 1966 in Fresno, California.

By the time I saw the light of day, both my grandfather and grandmother had remarried, giving me a new set of step grandparents: Donna Allen who eventually became one of my guardian angels during my difficult childhood, and Raul Green with whom my mother and I lived.

Oddly, my birth was accompanied neither by excruciating pain nor screams of agony. Instead, I made my debut in the world without the anguish and distress most women suffer in childbirth.

"Margaret," my mother laughingly says, "I had a tummy ache, made a trip to the ladies room, and an hour later I was cuddling a beautiful, screeching infant with dark hair and the tiniest hands and feet I had even seen."

She told me I was draped in a lightweight pale pink blanket since Fresno Septembers are still rather hot. A matching hat was slipped on my head, and I was carried back to my grandmother Vivian and step-grandfather Raul's home to begin life.

My mother was just sixteen years old—a child trying to nurture and rear a child of her own. The situation was rendered even more challenging when she and my dad parted ways and divorced even before I saw the light of day.

My grandparents' house was a modest, white stucco three-bedroom California ranch dwelling with a characteristic shallow pitch hipped roof that extended over a single car garage. Typical of the era, it was asymmetrical in design with an elongated almost to the ground appearance.

Flooring consisted of non-descript linoleum in the kitchen and solid wall to wall carpeting in the other areas of the house.

Dark wood paneled walls and floral patterned chairs presented a retro look, well before fifties' decorating was the trend. In another words, for the mid-sixties the house was already considered dated and rehab ready.

Although psychedelic crib sets were in vogue at the time, I slept in a more muted crib under which *Pepe* and *Louie*, a pair of overly vivacious non-stop-yapping, personality type A, high-strung Chihuahuas soon moved. Voluntarily, they assumed the role of 'body guard-guardian angels,' a responsibility they did not take lightly.

"Whenever anyone entered the nursery to see you," my mother told me, chuckling, "*Pepe* and *Louie* would jump out, ears and tails at attention, lips opened and curled exhibiting their full sets of pearly whites, snarling and growling. They would stop long enough just to spring forward and nip at the intruder's toes or ankles."

I clearly visualized this exciting scenario every time my mother spoke about *Pepe* and *Louie*. She didn't have the faintest inkling why they were so defensive and protective—perhaps they had a special canine intuition—an eerie premonition of what was to come and how powerless I would be to fight back.

Shortly thereafter, my mother packed up and we moved to my grandfather Chet and step-grandmother Donna's house in Oceanside, California. My memories of this period are non-existent since I was just a toddler. But family photos provide testimony of a loving environment in which I was held in their arms or seated on their laps and doted upon in a manner that is every child's right.

However, two years after my birth at eighteen years of age, my mother remarried, and on December 31, 1968 brought my sister Cindy into the world. In contrast to my dark locks at birth, my little 'New Year's Eve' sis had snow white hair, pale skin and huge luminous blue eyes. Wrapped in a white wool blanket, she looked like a tiny porcelain doll, so easy to love and cherish.

My mother's second marriage took place in Mexico and was immediately filled with insurmountable obstacles and irreconcilable conflicts. The young bride discovered her new husband had a wife and children in the States. Consequently, the newly weds did not set up home together. Ill-equipped to either deal with or resolve the menacing issues, she and my step-dad had the marriage annulled.

Thankfully, we were living with my grandmother Donna, a true guardian angel and kindhearted, loving woman willing and able to see the good in everyone. Rarely, if ever, did she speak ill or in an uncomplimentary manner of another human being. Her company was delightful and her compassion helped me overcome my first struggle with rejection.

During evening meals I would have a comfortable seat on her lap much to the envy of her own children who would often chastise her for spoiling me. Of course, I enjoyed the attention, unaware of the criticism Grandma was getting on my behalf.

Her one fault, to which her demise eventually could be attributed, was a nasty chain-smoking habit. I can remember entering a room and seeing her seated amidst billows of grey smoke that seemed to float in circles. Sadly, even the most conscientious oral and personal hygiene could not eliminate the odor of tobacco on her breath and clothes.

A dainty, small woman, Donna wore her short-bob cropped, thick red hair meticulously coiffed. She was one of those women whose scrupulous look was accomplished with a palm full of shampoo and a blow dryer, in an apparently skillful hand. Somehow, she always maintained an impeccable appearance.

Since pant suits were new on the fashion palette, Grandma Donna abandoned her dresses and skirts for trousers, obviously forgoing the sizzling trend of hot-pants and thigh-high boots, favored by the less than style conscious baby boomers. Her make-up was flawless, artistically applied with practiced strokes to enhance the already attractive features decorating her face.

Best of all—her sweet personality and ability to love and nurture were a novelty for a small child all too familiar with the sourness of emotional deprivation. It was a joy to live in such warm surroundings. However, I had no idea just how short-lived my idyllic lifestyle would be.

Soon after my mother, Cindy and I moved into a tight one bedroom apartment.

Denied child support from both husbands, besides holding a full time day job, my mother was obliged to work evenings at the Valley Drive-In on West Mission Avenue in Oceanside, to supplement her income. A single mom with two toddlers to nourish and clothe, the finances were never sufficient. She lived from paycheck to paycheck, sometimes wondering how she would pay the bills.

Debuting in the late thirties with one screen, The California 'auto theatre' had expanded to include four by the mid sixties.

Outdoor entertainment was now the trend, verified by the multi-colored pattern of endless parked cars in various sizes and designs, parked on Mission Avenue in the evenings. Often the theatre looked like a full to capacity, used car lot.

During this period my grandfather Chet who suffered from chronic heart disease, passed away. The heartbreaking event occurred shortly before my fourth birthday. A loving personality, his genuine smile and gentile presence were missed. It was a terrible loss for the family.

Even though he did not live with us, I loved him and always enjoyed the time I spent with him and my step-grandmother, Donna. Losing the love of her life, the grieving widow neither forgot her spouse nor remarried. Instead, she selflessly dedicated herself to the care of her children and me.

Life became exceedingly more challenging for a single woman with two children. Eventually, my mother was unable to face her obligations alone. Overwhelmed and anxious, when loneliness set in, she turned her attentions to a man with whom she worked at the Valley Drive-In.

George was a postal carrier by day, who tried to earn extra money with a second job at the theatre. Tall and lanky, his slender elongated face was highlighted by the dark-rimmed coke bottle glasses snugly tucked behind large slender ears. His vision was somewhat compromised, causing him to squint his blue-green eyes and crease his forehead. Though still a young man, his hairline had receded severely, drawing attention to his prematurely furrowed brow.

What sparse strands of hair he had were thin and not well kempt. I often wondered if Uncle George ever shampooed, and if so, why his hair was always so greasy. Looking back, I remember that he just didn't give the impression of a man attentive to personal appearance and cleanliness.

Furthermore, the stomach-turning odor of tobacco on his clothes and breath and the deep yellow stains on his teeth and right hand fingers betrayed his four packs a day Marlboro addiction. Simply stated, Uncle George was unattractive—or more appropriately put, rather unpleasant to focus the eyes on.

Uncle George was not necessarily a man of his times—a characteristic reflected in his unconventional sense of style. Forsaking the vibrantly colored polyester leisure suits and bell bottoms of the era, he dressed in somber shirts and snug fitting ankle hugging pants that practically fit the description of capris! *Groovey* and *funky* certainly did not describe the nerdy, fashion-blind 'Uncle George.'

Suffering from a bout of polio, thankfully not leaving visible traces, my mother's new boyfriend had been adopted as a young child. Uncertain of his roots, he knew absolutely nothing about his birth parents. Yet, despite his failings, during their courtship he exhibited a very pleasant and caring personality obviously trying to win the favor of not only my mother, but her two daughters.

"Margaret, Cindy," he would ask, grinning, "who wants ice cream?" Before we would answer and without even pausing to breathe, he'd croon, dangling the car keys, "Come on—let's go for ice cream." Delighted and giggling I would grab his hand, skipping all the way to the car.

Uncle George was kind and seemed to enjoy the company of children. He took us on many fun outings and tried to satisfy our wishes. This was such a radical change from my mom's second husband; and thrilled, I dared not think anything would ever change.

Sometimes there are nonverbal ways of communicating that enable children to get the message loud and clear even if interpreted with their own naive mindset. And for a four year old who had already been forced to taste the bitter tang of rejection, receiving Uncle George's doting attentions equated with being loved and wanted. It was a satisfying sensation, and I liked how nice and warm it made me feel.

After a short courtship, my mother took her third walk down the aisle, once again promising to love and honor a man until death would part them. She was twenty-one years old. Since I had fond feelings for Uncle George, I was beyond elated at the thought he would be living with us.

"Mom," I blurted when I heard the news, "is Uncle George going to live with us?"

"Yes, Margaret," she responded, her dark eyes glowing with the enthusiasm of a new bride, "yes, Uncle George is your new Dad."

Standing on my toes, I swirled around like a ballerina preparing her final curtsy. Giggling and breathless with excitement, I darted out of the room. I had to tell Cindy the good news—we had a Dad. And best of all, it was funny-looking, kind Uncle George! I had my first taste of happiness.

Obviously, the one bedroom apartment I shared with Mom and Cindy would no longer accommodate a family of four. At this point we needed a bigger house. After several house-hunting trips, Uncle George announced he had found the perfect place.

"Pack up," he said one evening right before dinner, "we're moving." He glanced at my mother, smiled and let out a sigh of relief. It wasn't much fun being sandwiched with three other people in a one-bedroom apartment.

Excited by the news, we packed up our personal belongings which weren't very many, got into the car and drove to our new home on a busy chaotic street buzzing with the activity of life.

"Which house is it?" I asked impatiently. Uncle George's response was blotted out by the clamor of horns honking as he lowered the widow to flick out his cigarette butt. I leaned forward from the rear seat eager to get a breath of air that didn't reek of tobacco. I was greeted by a late afternoon breeze which swept across my face, offering me a momentary reprieve from the throat-burning Marlboro air.

Uncle George turned off Montezuma Road and onto the heavily congested and equally hectic, four lane College

Avenue. From the sounds and chaos it was evident this street was a major traffic hub.

"Just a few more moments," he said trying to speak while balancing a lit cigarette between his lips. There was so much smoke in the car I could barely see the outline of his head from the back seat. "We're almost there."

Uncle George slowed down then gradually pulled into a driveway. The 1960 blue Volkswagen Beetle, aka 'Bug' rolled a few inches before coming to a full stop. "We're here," Uncle George blurted. "This is our new home."

He jumped out of the car just as my mother opened her door, stepped out and quickly went towards the rear to help Cindy and me get out. Once on our feet Uncle George walked us to the front door, inserted a key in the lock and pulled open the door. We heard it creak a bit despite the ruckus of honking horns and tires passing at full velocity.

"I guess I'd better grease these hinges," Uncle George said, laughing. My mother was impatient to step inside. "Let's get settled in, first," she responded reaching for my hand with her left hand, and Cindy's with her right before crossing the chipped walnut threshold.

The white stucco ranch house was amazingly similar to the one I had lived in previously with my grandparents. I guess they were all part of the fifties conformity building clone-like track-home trend. They were cost-effective, rectangular structures with centrally positioned entry doors built under low eaves topped with gabled roofs. Ours was no different. It had quite a good sized front lawn in the initial stages of blooming, and as I later learned, a rather spacious back yard encircled by a five-foot brown wood fence that creaked whenever it was opened.

A small, three bedroom house it was spartanly decorated with fifties era furnishings. Once inside, my eyes roamed around the living room settling on the TV, snuggly incased in an oak cabinet.

"Mom," I asked, puzzled, pointing in the direction of the wide-spread rabbit ears, "what's that funny thing on top of the TV?"

"Oh, just the antenna," she replied. "It makes the pictures easier to see." Not really understanding the explanation, I turned my attention to the kitchen. I walked in noticing an indefinable aroma which I later learned was characteristic of vacant homes.

Standing on top of an off-white, highly polished linoleum floor stood a white oval Formica-top table. A thick aluminum band encircled and hugged the upper portion. Neatly tucked under the table were four off-white vinyl chairs.

We settled in, and life with Uncle George promised to be what every child wishes for—fun and exciting, in a happy, peaceful environment. It was expected to be not quite the American dream, but the intermission between the Prologue and Act I.

Then the curtain fell. There were neither rounds of applause nor bows of recognition. Worst of all, the leading man, Uncle George, seemed to have mysteriously 'disappeared.' Though present physically, he was absent in every other way. His 'stand in,' who looked like him, was an entirely different person—at least to a young child unable to differentiate and understand severe behavioral changes.

Suddenly, like a rapidly sliding cloud concealing the sun's light, Uncle George was no longer available. His gracious, giving personality and desire to please seemed to switch off. Impatient, distant and always sour, he no longer had time for us.

Trips to the ice cream shop or park were first rare, then non-existent. Eventually, playful moments and happy echoes of hearty laughs turned into pouting moods, sulking sighs and grouchy grunts.

Deeply in love with my mother when they married, Uncle George soon found himself compromised and living with a woman who, much as she tried, could not return the fervor of his sentiment. However, for the sake of her children she was determined to make this "I do" work.

But her efforts did little to alter the nature of her union. There were neither demonstrations of affection on her part nor any special attention paid to a man who had rescued her and her two children from practically dire economic straits.

Disenchanted, and overwhelmed by the pressing demands of his new home purchase, the instant family he inherited but was having difficulty affording, and the financial responsibility to his widowed mother as well as his postal job and management position at the Valley Drive-In, Uncle George folded emotionally and physically.

Although never abusive to my mother, he started spanking Cindy and me when we did not conform to his behavioral rules. Chatty and never at a loss for words, I somehow got on Uncle George's nerves. One day I was arguing with Cindy while he was trying to watch TV.

"Cindy, that's my game, not yours," I yelled at my little sister, trying to snatch the board from her hands.

"No, Margaret," she snapped, "it belongs to me." I persisted, screaming at her in my high-pitched voice.

"Margaret," Uncle George snarled, "can you keep quiet for five minutes?"

"OK, Uncle George," I agreed, shouting back at Cindy. Aggravated and enraged, he repeated his command. "Be quiet Margaret! Didn't you hear what I said?"

The bickering continued. Cindy was in tears, and I was at her non-stop like most siblings playing together. Uncle George was on his feet with lightening speed. Grabbing me by the shoulders, he lifted me to my feet and slid me over to his chair. Breathing heavily, he sat and pulled me down until I hung over his knee. Fearful, yet not knowing why, I began to sob.

"Quiet," he shouted, "I said be quiet!" He raised his arm and swung it down open palm on my derrière. Stunned by the swatting echo and the sudden burning pain, I howled even louder. Besides the hurt, I was shocked and frightened by the dreadful experience of my first spanking. Sadly it would not be my last.

Uncle George had his own mentality regarding child rearing and social customs. He believed girls should wear dresses when not playing in the yard. I remember without nostalgia, the cotton or nylon white slips we wore under our dresses. They were a kind of uniform that doubled as a nightgown every afternoon when we took out naps.

Uncle George was also of the opinion and that Cindy and I, like all children should be seen and not heard.

Therefore, when in the company of other adults, it was required for us to look nice and sit still on the couch without squirming or opening our mouths. Any and all disobedient actions were punishable and treated with spankings—even for a couple of toddlers!

"Where is Uncle George?" I asked my mother, scared by this 'bad man' I no longer recognized.

"What happened to Uncle George?" I asked over and over. "Where is the kind, smiling man who played with me and Cindy and was always so delighted to see us? And who is this angry man who always hits us?"

"Margaret," my mother responded, visibly annoyed, "we are very lucky to have someone willing to put a roof over our heads, pay the bills and feed us. We could be worse off, running around barefoot and starving in a third world country!" I had absolutely no idea what she was talking about—it all went over my head and did little to settle the confusion within me.

"I miss Uncle George," I whispered, sobbing silently before drifting off to sleep.

Though not yet five years of age, I started kindergarten. Delighted to be in an environment with lots of other children, I went to school each morning enthusiastically and willingly. Once Uncle George had turned into a fearful *Jekyll* and *Hyde* personality, I was eager to be away from home as much as possible.

School represented a timeout from the intimidating home environment and an opportunity to socialize and play with children my own age. I was at liberty to laugh and talk without the threat of screams and spankings.

At the end of the day dinner was served and consumed

around the Formica-top table, family style. In keeping with Uncle George's 'parenting philosophy,' Cindy and I dined in silence unless we were invited to speak. This was a rare event and most of the time it seemed as if Cindy and I were just two table decorations all dressed up in our pastel cotton dresses.

My mother and Uncle George rarely engaged each other in conversation, and the atmosphere was often tense. Dinner was not an enjoyable event that I looked forward to at day's end.

Budget constraints dictated most of the menu selections. However, my mother did the best she could to prepare the macaroni and cheese or hot dog and hamburger dishes she served nightly. Soda was prohibited; therefore, we had a tall glass of milk to complement the meal.

Uncle George believed we should consume healthier diets and would periodically insist on having Brussels sprouts, broccoli or cabbage on the table. Vegetables were not exactly our preference, as with the majority of children, but he would sit with a stern look and oblige me and Cindy to eat.

"I want you to finish everything on your plates! Do you understand?" he would say, irritated, and not waiting for a response—"Eat it all—every bit of it!"

Many times we would stuff ourselves beyond the comfort level for fear of feeling Uncle George's hand heavily whack out derrières. To avoid the pain we ate until we were physically sick, ran to the bathroom and vomited. "Margaret, Cindy you are lucky to have food on the table, and don't you ever forget it," Mom would say before we were bathed and told to go to bed.

There were neither endearing rituals nor affectionate traditions. We were never read any bedtime stories, and no word was ever mentioned about the existence of God or the comfort of prayer. Religion didn't exist in the minds of Uncle George and my mother—at least not where children were concerned.

The only one who seemed to care about us was Greta, a beautiful former police German Shepherd with alert dark eyes, a shiny coat and a seemingly endless pink tongue that felt hot and moist whenever she licked our hands or faces. I would giggle, especially when she ran her tongue over my toes as I played with Cindy in the back yard, teasing her by pulling my foot away from her face.

Greta was everything my mother and Uncle George weren't—loving, attentive and protective; a baby sitter, a guardian and a faithful playmate.

My mother was stressed out from working, frustrated from her constant spats with Uncle George and far too frazzled and exhausted to have any energy left for her children. To add to the distress Uncle George took on a third job as newspaper carrier. Unhappily, this involved the whole family. My mother would drive the car, and Uncle George would toss the papers out the window as we passed the houses.

Since there was no baby-sitter available, Cindy and I were lifted from our beds at threeAM every morning and awakened shortly thereafter, finding ourselves in the back seat of the Beetle Bug covered with mounds of smelly newspapers. The stench nauseated me. By the time we returned home, I had black ink all over my hands, face and pajamas and greeted the day with an upset stomach.

Eventually, my mother's less than wholesome lifestyle resulted in chronic bouts of depression. It was not unusual to see her head for the bedroom sobbing and shut the door for privacy. Later I noticed her eyes were bloodshot and puffed and her skin took on a flushed tint. She walked with rounded shoulders and her head lowered in an almost unnatural position, often dragging her feet—a demeanor that betrayed her misery.

To intensify the dreary mood, my grandmother had passed away. I remember my mother sitting at the Formica-top table, crying with her head buried in her hands. Her body was shaking as her loud piercing sobs seemed to echo through the house. I felt sad for her, though I really didn't understand much about death except for the fact I would never see my grandmother again.

Uncle George did not accompany my mother to the funeral, obliging her to attend alone. In keeping with his rigid parenting rules, Cindy and I were not permitted to participate in Grandma's funeral because it was not an appropriate place for children.

Remaining often without the maternal attention we craved, Cindy and I began to fight each other to get Mom to notice us. We became fierce competitors in the quest for love often exasperating my mother by our constant presence. She no longer had any peace or privacy. When she dressed for work we were there vying for her attention, giggling as she slipped a stiff Dacron pastel shirtwaist over her head and slid her feet into thin midsized heeled shoes. When she puttered around the kitchen we sat playing and more often than not, arguing nearby. We were two pesky little devils—children desperate for some love and affection.

The situation with Uncle George worsened. The spankings were frequent and seemed to hurt more. Shouts were louder and lasted longer. I was frightened every time I saw him coming. By now it was sheer misery to be in his company.

If I talked I got yelled at—"Can't you be quiet for five minutes, Margaret!" I was full of energy and loved to dance around the room singing at full voice, often imitating a child opera star who I had heard on the radio. However, my exuberance and creativity were repeatedly met with punishments.

"Mom," I asked one day in tears, "can Uncle George go away? He always hits me for everything. If I sing and dance I get spanked, and if I talk I get yelled at and sent to my room. I don't like Uncle George. I don't want him to live with us anymore."

Her response was a shrug of the shoulders, a forlorn gaze and a deep, prolonged sigh. She quickly turned her head, but not before I caught sight of a tear rolling down her cheek.

Chapter 2

The Wickedness of Man

*"When the Lord saw that the wickedness of man
on the earth was great, and that man's every
thought and all the inclination of his heart were
only evil, he regretted that he had made man on
the earth and was grieved to the heart."*
—Genesis 6:5

His groping hand invaded from behind, selfishly, illicitly.
When a cold finger surged forward, poking at my skin, I
twitched, then froze even though his breath shot out in
irregular spurts, loud and hot on my neck. The pain was
quick, unexpected and piercing. I held my own breath, a
reaction not uncommon in a defenseless five-year-old
child, facing a terrifying, life-altering moment.

The trickle of blood felt warm, almost ticklish, as it
oozed down my legs. "Put on your underwear," John
whispered gruffly, apparently frightened by the sound of
Uncle George's Beetle coming to a full stop in the driveway. The Volkswagen Bug was well known for its noisy
motor, setting off an alarm to warn the culprit my parents

had returned. It signaled his 'babysitting' job was completed for that evening.

"Hurry Margaret," John urged, breathless, unconcerned about the innocence he had just stolen and perhaps exaggeratedly undisturbed by the emotional and physical pain and anguish inflicted as a consequence of his criminal behavior. "Your parents are here—get dressed. Let's go meet them at the door!"

Dazed and scared by what had happened, I was far too young and naive to process the severity of the violation committed against me. Grabbing my panties from John's outstretched waving hand, I slipped them on, watching as the sliding drops of blood stained them a bright crimson.

Looking down, I noticed a small splattering on the white linoleum floor. John caught my lowered gaze. Immediately, he bent over and swept his hand over the smudge, eventually clearing the 'evidence' with a brusque finger sweep down the leg of his striped multi-colored bell-bottom pants.

"Come on, Margaret," he blurted, snatching my hand and dragging me to the door. It hurt when I walked and the burning continued, becoming worse when I made *pee pee*. Noticing it was red instead of yellow scared me, but even too terrorized to tell anyone, I kept it to myself.

The throbbing hurt made my eyes swell with tears. It was a very different gnawing hurt—so unlike the sore throats or tummy aches I had felt before.

"Don't cry, now," John whispered, bending his head down to my ear. He brushed his arm across my face to catch the droplets before they ran down my cheeks betraying his awful secret.

As we headed toward the door, John noticed I was walking slower, practically dragging my feet while touching myself with my free hand. With my childish ingenuity I believed I could actually caress away the agonizing ache.

"Stop doing that," he said, irritated. "Grownups do this all the time. You don't want to behave like a silly little girl. Do you?" he questioned, sneering.

"No," I responded, focusing my gaze away from him.

I turned my head in the direction of Uncle George's big, unsightly recliner chair in which, according to John, I had become an 'adult.' Upholstered with a burnt orange and brown coarse plaid fabric, it seemed to have springs of aluminum beneath its old, notched wood frame.

Once the chair was set in motion, there was never the possibility of a squeak-free rock. John was a good looking young guy with dark, curly hair. A pair of large blue eyes enhanced his olive complexion. A relative through marriage, he was often referred to as Uncle John and seemed like a serious, responsible teen.

As soon as he entered the house, he'd dart directly for the recliner, settle in comfortably and with a gesture of his psychedelically clothed arm, he'd beckon me to come sit beside him to watch TV.

This was the setting every time for the unlawful acts of sexual molestation John subjected me to for many years. They started with touching and progressed until he actually drew blood.

Once I was in Uncle George's chair, the scenario was always the same. Unbuttoning my dress, he'd lift it over my head, then slip his index finger into the waist-band of my panties and yank them down.

"Margaret," he'd say coyly, "you're so vivacious and out-going, I know you want to act like an adult. Don't you want to have fun like the grownups do?" I acknowledged his question with a nod which he interpreted as a yes. Having what he twisted into 'consent,' he proceeded to ask for a 'hand job.'

Gazing up at him through puzzled eyes only encouraged him to take my hand and place it where it would give him pleasure. "I'm going to show you what it means to be an adult, Margaret. It's very easy and you'll like it. Just do as I say."

Unable to understand what was happening and unaware he was assaulting me with potentially harmful deceptions, I followed all John's instructions as he led me through some rudimentary stages of foreplay and oral sex. I had no idea what I was doing, but believed I was learning how to be an 'adult.' To make it more enticing, he egged me on, encouraging me to fantasize he was a lollipop.

"Margaret, if you do this you will grow up quicker and no longer have to act like a child," was his cunning 'seduction strategy.' The thought of growing up dangled tantalizingly in front of me. It was thrilling—after all, what youngster doesn't want to be an adult overnight? Furthermore, the quicker I grew up, the sooner I could leave Uncle George—and even as a small child, this was my ultimate goal.

John was clever in his subtly sweet coercion, just as most sexual predators are when trying to catch the attention and complicity of their innocent prey. They know the right words and are savvy persuaders, convincing and agreeable.

After awhile I discovered that whenever the Beetle pulled into the driveway, John would instinctively shift into 'panic mode.' He'd abruptly stop the 'grown-up' activity, adjust his pants and send me to my room to get dressed. The pattern was repeated each time, and as the years passed, I began to understand something was not quite right.

If we were not doing anything wrong, I often questioned, why was I forbidden to tell anyone about my games and 'lessons' with John? Why did we have to stop every time my mom and Uncle George returned home? They were adults!

After each molestation episode he made me promise I would never reveal 'our big secret'; it was something very special just between Uncle John and me. Looking me directly in the eyes, he would 'threaten,' "Margaret, if you tell your parents, I will no longer help you grow up. You will remain a child and have to stay here with Uncle George!"

His crafty blackmail worked. A sheepish grin gave him the green light to continue the indecent liberties he took with me. The truth was I believed every word my cool Uncle John said. Yet the stark reality was—when he started violating me, I was just a few years older than a toddler.

However, thankfully, John's misdeeds came to an end before he could complete the sex act. One evening, slowed by his own selfish passions, he was not swift enough to cover up the 'crime scene.' Therefore, when Uncle George spotted him pulling up his pants as he walked through the front door, John was caught red-handed.

There were no questions asked, and no defense plausible—it was more than evident my babysitter had sexually molested me. The sole unknown was that he had been doing it almost three years.

When questioned about the blood stains on my panties, I told my mother in tears, "I fell and hurt myself while Uncle John was teaching me to ride my bicycle without training wheels." I lied because I knew I could not share 'our special secret' with her. John would be upset—but more importantly I would not be able to act like an adult and leave Uncle George.

In school I was an energetic, outgoing, vivacious student with the gift of gab. I was friendly, liked people and had a flagrant need to communicate. Consequently, when it was time for evaluations, my teachers always chastised me for unruly, disorderly and disruptive behavior.

One of my first friends in second grade was Mary Fleuret, a very bright little French girl with brown, waist-length straight hair, dazzling blue eyes and a fair, flawless complexion. Quiet, and obedient in class, she was in total contrast with my vibrant, bubbling personality.

Mary's family seemed to perfectly fit my idea of the ideal family. They were gracious, young, attractive individuals who resided in a large bi-level home on a copiously tree-lined street in an up-scale neighborhood. The Fleurets' front lawn was lush and flourishing; each meticulously mowed blade of emerald green grass seemed to beam in the sunlight.

When the dew drops settled, the lawn seemed to be generously sprinkled with diamonds. Several groupings of multi-colored flowers in various stages of bloom accentu-ated the already appealing entrance of the residence. The

Fleurets lived in the American dream house—so idyllic and inviting it appeared to be perfect.

Mary's parents were a loving couple, unafraid to demonstrate their affection for each other and their children, so unlike the arctic, distant and tense environment in my family. There were genuine and frequent exchanges of hugs and kisses and an ever endearing feeling of agreement and availability—so amazingly welcoming.

I received many kind weekend invites from Mary's parents, and the visits were such a respite from my own unhappy life. Mrs. Fleuret always prepared a delicious meal which was enjoyed by the family, united around a beautifully set rectangular French provincial dining room table.

On numerous occasions, after dinner Mr. Fleuret would lift the ivory linen napkin from his lap, pat his lips to eliminate all traces of the wonderful meal he had enjoyed, and gently fold it in half before placing it to the left of his dessert plate. Smiling broadly, he'd say, "Mary, go get a game we can all play together."

"OK, Daddy," she lisped, flashing a grin that revealed two missing front teeth and the reason for her often amusing speech.

Emulating her dad, she rolled her napkin, quickly setting it on the table as she was taught. Sliding off the cushioned dark-wood bench, she skipped out of the room to get the game.

While Mary was searching for the game of her choice, Mrs. Fleuret collected the soiled plates, glasses and cutlery. Returning, she swept the table and hand-stitched place mats with several quick hand movements, careful to collect the bread crumbs in her free palm before heading back to the kitchen.

When the evening clean-up was completed, she joined the family who eagerly awaited her return to start playing.

I loved visiting the Fleurets. Neither scolded nor ordered to 'be seen and not heard,' I was accepted by them for who I was—a sprightly, capricious little girl who just liked to talk; a love-starved child who craved attention and the company of others. And with Mary and her family, I was able to fill the hollow vacuum growing within, even if momentarily.

Towards the end of second grade after one of our hurried, uneventful dinners in which no one either greeted or spoke to another, Uncle George announced, clearing his throat, "We're moving. We're going to live in Carlsbad."

"Where is that, Daddy?" I chirped, curious to know where I was going.

"It's about a fifteen-minute ride from here," he grunted, lighting a cigarette.

I didn't know what was worse—the odor of sulfur tickling my nose when he struck the match, or the stench of tobacco and seared cigarette paper turning my stomach when he exhaled his first full puff. Both made me feel a bit queasy and lightheaded. Holding my breath, I coughed several times, perhaps believing the action of my chest heaving up and down would eliminate the uncomfortable, unsettled feeling.

Uncle George and my mother purchased another tan-wood, shingled track home with a dark asphalt shingled roof, in Carlsbad, California. Unlike the previous homes, this one was brand new. Measuring twenty-two hundred feet, it was somewhat larger than the others and built with four bedrooms and the luxury of two baths.

Uncle George gave the College Avenue house to his mother, which was the motive for our move. We took our furnishings, including the horrendous burnt orange and brown plaid recliner chair. With it the recurrent memoirs of my stolen innocence tailgated me like the ominous black shadows trailing a storm.

Weeks and months passed with reckless speed. I was now in the fourth grade, and my father, Uncle George, thought it wise that I learn how to read, write and speak Spanish. Enrolled in the bi-lingual program, my new class-mates were immigrant Hispanic children who spoke little if any English. At the time it was a traumatic experience to be pulled from my neighborhood friends and immersed in a radically diverse cultural environment.

The Mexican students were segregated in the school because of their language difficulties. I felt uprooted and misplaced—an outsider in a room overpopulated with unfamiliar faces and unrecognizable sounds.

"I don't belong here," I repeated to myself every morning, dreading another day of classes. To add salt in the wound—I was mercilessly teased by the neighborhood children for being seated with kids who didn't speak a word of English.

However, according to 'wise' Uncle George, my tenure in the bi-lingual program would serve as a 'lesson learning penance.' Not only would I obtain fluency in another language, but I would be forced to stop chattering since no one would understand what I was saying.

Classes were filled with underprivileged foreigners; young boys and girls alien to American soil, but not to poverty and hardship. They were children living in lack and deprivation whose parents had immigrated to the USA for a chance at a better, more dignified life. Their sons and daughters would receive the education they were denied, and they would find decent-paying jobs granting them the possibility to take care of their young growing families.

Uncle George was certain that removing me from a middle-class environment in which kids lived in nice comfortable homes and wore trendy clothes would instill in me an appreciation for what I had. Plus, as a bonus, I would learn Spanish.

Maria Gomez, handpicked by Uncle George, was my teacher, since he found complicity in her regarding disciplinary tactics.

Mrs. Gomez was a *petite* curvaceous, middle-aged woman with a short-cropped, dark hairdo accentuating her Latin heritage. Meticulous about her appearance, she dressed stylishly with matching shoes and impeccably applied make-up. Gold chains, shiny multiple bangle bracelets and medium sized gold hoop earrings added glimmer to her look.

At a certain point of the day, depending on the season, a direct ray of sunlight would sneak into the room and beam its glow in her direction, illuminating her like an overly decorated Christmas tree suddenly switched on.

Neither exasperated nor intimidated by my energetic personality, the high-strung, temperamental Latina, Mrs. Gomez, was quite adept at handling me.

"Margaret," she said in her heavily accented English, "you can talk all you want in class, as long as you do it in Spanish." *I can talk all I want—that is a new turn of events*, I thought to myself. It suited me just fine. In less than a year I learned Spanish!

In fifth grade my extroverted nature once again decided my fate. Uncle George was summoned and forced to listen to Mrs. Gomez's lamentations about my troublesome and unsettling behavior in class.

"Mrs. Gomez," Uncle George said, without the faintest trace of even a courteous smile, "we need to stop this problem. You have my permission to spank Margaret with a belt whenever she becomes disorderly in class. This is the only thing kids understand and the only way to teach them manners."

If nothing else, Uncle George was consistent. At home he was beating me religiously, unflinching in his administering of punishment. Although my grades were good academically, in comportment I received an unsatisfactory—a judgment based on my incessant chatting during lessons. The sentence was always the same—punishment with the belt. It started in the third grade and became more ferocious as I grew older.

Once Mrs. Gomez gave him the report, he was ready to 'discipline' me that evening.

"Margaret, go to your room right now and wait for me," he said, flashing me a callous accusatory glance that dug deep into me, even before the stiff cold leather hit my skin. This was part of his tormenting punishment. Like a condemned woman on death row, waiting minute by minute for justice, my agony was prolonged by him, sometimes for hours. I knew what to expect and would have preferred to have it delivered quickly and be over and done with until the next time.

But this was not Uncle George's 'penalty strategy.' Instead, he'd have me wait from minutes to hours believing it intensified the 'procedure.' From the time I was seven the punishment always had been the same.

Walking into my room, he'd say, "Margaret, take off your underwear and clothes." Before finishing the sentence, he'd angrily tug the tip of his belt back, free it from the square gold buckle, and with a sudden brusque movement, zap it through the confining loops along the waistband of his pants.

He approached like a hunter nearing his prey, hurled himself on the bed, and grabbed my arm, flinging me over his knees with my *derrière* facing the ceiling. Once I was in the desired position, I felt a quick draft when he lifted his arm, just seconds before the sharp rigid leather grazed my bare skin. The lashes were ten in number and ten plus in severity.

Even my howls and sobs did little to alleviate the excruciating pain and absolutely nothing to turn a callous tyrant into a compassionate parent.

"You have to learn how to behave," he shouted as he decorated the surface of my delicate back, *derrière* and thighs with huge open welts. "Margaret, I'm doing this for your own good. You have to stop being so outgoing and stop talking—Mrs. Gomez says you talk … talk… talk too much. Do you understand? Do you? " he screamed, pushing me off his lap.

I noticed his sallow complexion flushed. His face was moistened from the circular beads of perspiration gliding from his forehead down his cheeks before settling on his curled upper lip. I knew Uncle George was furious—the irrational violence was his ruthless traitor.

"Get dressed. You must stay in your room," were Uncle George's post-beating orders. I was on restriction, which meant I was in solitary, in my own room. Not permitted to see or talk to anyone, I was my own company.

My mother never once came to dry my tears, give me a hug or see how badly Uncle George had beaten me. If I needed comfort or medical attention, it was not her concern. My shouts and cries, plus the wafting echo of the belt digging into my skin were indisputable evidence I had been brutally abused by her husband.

That evening as every other, I crawled into bed, wincing in pain as my bruised body hit the cool sheets. The bloody sores stuck to my pajamas, intensifying the agony whenever I tried to find a less torturous position.

Trembling as if suffocated by an intangible force I could not recognize, I lay awake, paralyzed by the throbbing hurt—both physical and emotional. The minutes ticked away with nonchalant lethargy—a privilege of idle hours. I cried myself to sleep.

After years of severe belt whippings, my body in self-defense became numb as soon as the fifth lashing had left its bloody footprint. However, the day after, I felt stiff. A gnawing burning from my thighs all the way to my upper back made dressing myself agonizing.

In the seventies it was not considered unlawful to spank children or administer any form of non-life threatening corporal punishment; therefore, knowledge of such action was never reported to authorities or acted upon. Consequently, fully authorized to discipline me with physical violence, Mrs. Gomez and the school Principal were aware of my belt whippings. Thankfully, they both felt uncomfortable hitting me. Instead, Mrs. Gomez's remedy for misbehaving was 'pinch punishment.'

Although she was rather kind most of the time, when I went into chatty, disruptive mode she would prance right up to me, grab my skin directly under the arm with her thumb and index finger, yank it down as far as she could and twist it. I felt her nails imbedding into my skin. The pain was unbearably piercing. Afterwards, the huge irregular black and blue bruises were a month-long testament of her cruelty.

However, odd as it may seem, despite the 'pinch punishment,' Mrs. Gomez was actually a positive influence in my life. She was affectionate with me and really didn't like imparting lessons through pinching, but Uncle George had persuaded her to believe it was the only 'language' I understood.

Unlike my parents, Mrs. Gomez always embraced me with a hug after the pinch and assured me it was for my own good. Actually, thinking back, I remember she took an interest in my private life and was the only person Uncle George respected. Her intervention in the end redeemed me from prolonged and enduring physical abuse.

My mother, who attended the parent-teacher conferences along with Uncle George, merely listened in silence. Never expressing an opinion nor posing a question regarding my academic or behavioral progress in school, she seemed totally oblivious to anything that involved me. Her comments, thoughts and feelings were buried in a lethal silence of apathy.

Apparently disgusted with my outgoing personality, my mother turned a cold shoulder early on. There were neither fun bed-time stories, nor memorable bath or tucking in rituals with kisses and giggles that children look back on with tear-filled eyes and warm, endearing feelings. It almost seemed as if she were a spectator in someone else's life—watching from the sidelines without ever actually stepping into the limelight.

Fourth, fifth and sixth grades were pretty much the same. Beatings, 'pinch punishments' and lengthy periods of solitary restriction in my room. Outside school and my home, the neighborhood children continued to badger me and my family because of my enrollment in the Spanish program. They teased me relentlessly, poking fun at me for hanging out with the Hispanic children, especially since they were segregated in school.

They were also aware Uncle George was lashing me. "Margaret, your parents are weird," they would say, frowning with disdain. "Why do they beat you? What's wrong with them? Our parents don't hit us like that. Margaret this is crazy!"

I tried to conceal my pain and brushed off their comments, but deep down I felt a gut-wrenching twinge. Why was my life so different from all the other kids? Didn't they ever talk too much? Didn't their parents ever get mad at them for misbehaving? If so, why didn't they get hit for their own good?

I really didn't think I wanted answers to my questions—just because I secretly suspected I already had them. Furthermore, I had a feeling I was actually better off without answers.

Although I did not have friends, thankfully my grandmother, Donna Allen, cared enough about me to pick me up on Fridays after school and take me home to spend the weekend with her and her family. Of course, I was only permitted to accept her gracious invites if I was not grounded.

My grandmother had met Mrs. Gomez on several occasions and had expressed her disdain over Uncle George's violent disciplinary measures. She tried to intervene and nip his brutal beatings, but succeeded only in losing his respect and her privilege to have me over for the weekends. Threatened by her intervention and questioning of his parenting methods, he felt she represented an irreconcilable conflict, an issue which would prohibit him from rearing me as he sought fit.

Although Grandmother Donna was a wise, intelligent woman who more than demonstrated her love for me, she yielded under Uncle George's pressure, stepped aside and ceased to express her views, believing it was the most advantageous tactic to follow in order to continue her weekend relationship with me.

My grandmother, recently deprived of the love of her life, had a difficult time as a single parent with two children in tender age to rear. However, whenever I was her house guest, she would spoil me without limits. I was never asked to be seen and not heard and never disciplined. Instead, she told me I was special. She said she loved me for who I was, with my extroverted personality and penchant for chatting. She also emphasized there was nothing wrong with me, and I should recognize how special and gifted I was.

Grandma Donna never tried to stifle my bubbly, vivacious personality. Instead, she always encouraged me to accept who I was and just be myself. Never speaking ill of my parents, though warranted and justified, she did her best to compensate for the deprivation and lack at home by treating me with extra kindness and attention. Listening with interest and enthusiasm to all I said, she understood my familial situation, thus rectifying the misery by including me in her summer vacation plans. It was her very own special way of administering love.

A hard-working and conscientious full-time employee with a family to support, my grandmother loved to pack her rod, reel and go fishing for relaxation. Every year she rented a mobile home for two weeks on the beach and took us all surf-fishing.

Grandma's two children were a son Matt, and a daughter Andy who were somewhat older and often envious because their mom doted on me with almost exaggerated attention. At the table my place would be on her lap, and although we never fought they did have moments in which they expressed their anger. However, for the most part, the vacation went smoothly. Today, I have beautiful photos and endearing memories of the fun times together.

At the conclusion of sixth grade I graduated from elementary school, bidding farewell to Mrs. Gomez and my Hispanic classmates. Uncle George decided it was opportune to move his mother into our home and purchase another for the family. He was now working long hours to afford supporting his mother and family in addition to paying for and maintaining the new two-story residence in La Costa.

The new neighborhood was up-scale, and the big white stucco house sat pompously on an acre of land upon which multi-clusters of colorful flowers, saturated in the sun rays swayed in the winds. A bright red tile roof completed the post card-like attractiveness of the house.

Finally, Uncle George made the decision to trade in the chortling blue Beetle and drove home one evening in a 1975 white, two-door Ford Pinto with gaudy red vinyl interiors. Never having a fondness for luxury cars, he believed it was not necessary to drive around in expensive vehicles just to impress the neighbors.

Much as I despised it, I had to admit the Pinto was a definite improvement over the old beat up rejects he usually drove. His justification for getting behind the wheel of such unattractive cars most people destine for the junkyard was, "They take me where I want to go."

My mother, on the other hand, had purchased her first brand new set of wheels—a burgundy Honda Accord with sandy interiors. Apparently, my parents were on a spending spree. Thrilled about the house up-grade and the new vehicles, my mother and Uncle George decided to go 'all out' for new furnishings.

Since my mother favored the color green in an almost exaggeratedly obsessive way, she had green shag carpeting installed throughout the entire house except for my room and Cindy's. Although thankfully the walls remained white, all the furniture was upholstered in various shades of greens—it was like living in 'jolly green giant land.'

Besides being garish and aesthetically unappealing, the house was the basis of many scary nightmares that would awaken me from a deep sleep, drenched in sweat with my heart racing. It seemed to be invaded by demons—a haunted house that disturbed as much as the trauma and horrendous abuse I experienced while living there, leaving me tormented and terrified for many years thereafter.

I was not quite sure if I created the ghost that inhabited space within the walls of the house or if it was there prior to our arrival. However, the eerie, unexplained breezes and the caresses I would feel on my head, arms and back were very real sensations.

The house invaded my dreams, blazing through the images in a ball of fire, searing every thought and emotion. Crackling sounds and an excruciating heat would leave me soaked in perspiration and breathing heavily. It seemed as if the house was chasing after me, trying to trap and lock me within its walls permanently.

Paralyzed by fear, I had trouble catching my breath. However, the nightmare did not end when I awakened. It returned instead to ruthlessly haunt me for many years like a treacherous enemy, quieted only by the sweet flavor of a settled score.

The Book of Job

Chapter 3

The First Trial

"And the Lord said to Satan, 'Behold, all that
he has is in your power; only do not lay a hand
upon his person.' So Satan went forth from the
presence of the Lord."
—Job 1:12

I was now in seventh grade, my first year of junior high, and my sister Cindy was in fifth. We argued and shouted at each other, as most siblings do, but often tried to make an effort to co-exist as best we could. However, a loving sisterly relationship filled with alliance, solidarity and complicity was just not there.

Life in junior high took on a new twist. I now had seven different teachers to contend with—one for each subject. Unfortunately, this equated to seven recriminations for exaggerated talking and disruptive behavior in class.

Not long after school started, Uncle George was summoned for a conference and told seven times, in seven different voices, "Margaret is a very bright girl, but I cannot get her to stop the chattering. She talks continually, absolutely refuses to sit still in class and distracts the other students. Something has to be done!"

Uncle George, who had begun to drink profusely at this time, accepted the comments vehemently. That evening he was tense and more rigid than usual. Avoiding eye contact he said through gritted teeth, "Margaret, enough is enough. You are now on restriction until you stop talking in class and bring home a satisfactory report card. You will remain in your bedroom and leave only to attend school. Is that clear?"

I nodded as always, never really believing I would be able to remain silent for lengthy periods of time. In fact, I didn't, and as a result my restriction lasted for two whole years. Seven hundred thirty days alone in my room—the thought was horrifying!

But this time Uncle George wanted more than a nod. "Did you hear me?" he repeated, raising the volume of his voice.

Shifting my gaze away from his beet red face, I grunted an OK. I felt a terrible searing hatred rise from the pit of my stomach all the way up to my chest, like a rapid, out-of-control whirlpool. Breaking out in a cold sweat, I feared that if I looked at him he would see it pour out from my eyes. Terrified of his drunken rages, I knew I could not let him know how much I detested him.

If nothing else, Uncle George was consistent. The lashings were still his major disciplinary strategy. Oddly enough, on this occasion my mother intervened, though certainly not to halt the barbaric punishment.

As he yanked off his belt and shouted, "Take off your underwear and clothes—hurry it up, I have other more important things to do," she entered the room.

"George," she said, "you cannot make Margaret remove her underwear anymore. She is going to get her period soon."

How utterly 'considerate' of her to worry about my getting whipped naked—did she expect a thank-you after I was all bruised and sore? And what was the nature of her concern?

I considered this 'new privilege' as an opportunity to put on every item of underwear I owned foolishly believing it would lighten the pain. However, grunting and reeking of hard liquor to make my stomach turn, Uncle George beat me almost raw even if fully clothed. When he left with a smirk of satisfaction ingrained on his face, I buried my sadness in my trembling open palms and sobbed—"I hate you. I hate you. I wish you were dead. I wish you would die right now."

Part one was completed—I was lashed. Part two awaited—I was to be confined to my room.

During my restriction, I was allowed to come down and join the family for dinner, clean off the table and wash and dry the dishes. Afterwards, my 'freedom' privileges were revoked, and I was sent back to 'solitary confinement' in my room. Weekends were no exception—except I didn't go to school and the detention was round the clock.

Unlike the rest of the house, my room was not redecorated. The floor was a fifties white non-descript linoleum, easily defined as dull and just plain ugly. A twin bed mounted on a dull metal frame sat in the middle of the room.

Across from the bed was a single dark wood dresser that appeared to have seen better days. It was heavily notched and chipped, showing signs of wear and tear. Not permitted to tape on my walls, I hung pictures of my favorite singers and bands on the closet door. It was the only personal touch distinguishing the room from a vacant college dorm room—or worse.

I had no television, telephone, or distractions. My only visitors were the mice I would see and hear scurrying about the room. Their beady black eyes would sometimes glare at me in the semi-darkness of dusk. Arrogantly, they'd pass my bed, squeaking as if intentioned to torment me further. Instinctively, I'd lift my head to see what was happening—not really wanting to see anything.

Petrified of these tiny rodents with their skinny string tails, I'd grab a blanket and pillow from my bed and dart to the bathroom I shared with Cindy. Once I was certain the evening 'mice romp' had come to an end, I'd spend the night either in the tub or lying on a four foot counter, curled in the shape of a doughnut. Rolling up a towel, I shoved it under the door with my bare feet to prevent the ugly creatures from entering.

The following morning after a restless, sleepless night I ran crying, "Mom, I'm terrified—there are mice in my room! They come out and run all around chasing each other. Don't make me stay there all the time. I have to get in bed and stare at the ceiling because I'm sacred to put my feet on the floor. I know they will bite my ankles. Mom, I don't want to stay in that room!"

"OK, Margaret," she said in almost a hoarse whisper, I'll get some traps later and we'll catch them."

She kept her word. The traps were set. That evening I heard short, piercing squeaks and the repeated snap of metal on wood. Curious, I gazed down from my bed just in time to see what resembled a slaughterhouse filled with mice. Caught in the traps, their heads were practically severed from their bodies. Some of the tails continued to swish limply along the edge of the trap. Spots of still-fresh blood looked nearly black on the white linoleum. Nauseated, I was frozen in terror, my pajamas glued to my body with the droplets of my own perspiration.

The following evening my demons returned to haunt me. Asleep, I was suddenly awakened by the pressure of a warm hand resting on my forehead. It seemed to spring right through the wall against which the head of my bed stood. Mysteriously, it extended forward and settled on my head. Alone in the room, I knew of no reasonable explanation. Although I couldn't see it in the dark, I felt the staccato like pressure of finger pads prancing across my skin.

Again petrified by the strange, uncanny phenomenon, my first reaction was to run downstairs. However, the staircase was not a very solid structure. Each step was open and disconnected. I was afraid that the demons haunting me were hidden under the staircase waiting in the darkness to trip me on my way down.

To avoid serious injury, I ran at breakneck speed, almost flying, my feet barely tipping the steps. Years later, I 'learned' how to fly through the house in my dreams, to escape confrontations with the evil spirits.

After the 'flight' down the steps, my only choice was to return to my 'prison' and just wait it out, shuddering and crying myself to sleep.

My one release and possibility for normalcy occurred during the two hours before my parents returned from work every evening. As soon as I entered the house after school, I would either turn on the TV, or make a mad dash for the telephone and chat with my friends as every young schoolgirl does. However, hampered by presumed fading memories, few parents feel comfortable admitting to having either an understanding of or empathy for this particular 'rite of passage.'

The 'reprieve' was short lived and not without consequence. Since call waiting was nonexistent in the seventies, every time my mom or Uncle George tried to dial the number in lieu of Cindy's 'hello,' a busy signal would be their greeting.

Someone was on the phone! The red light flashed. My awful 'crime' was discovered. That evening I went to bed sobbing, bruised and in excruciating pain. Uncle George had whipped me again.

Exasperated by my restriction and Uncle George's lashings, I found an enjoyable outlet for my frustrations. Without the help or advice of an accomplice, I started to absent myself from art class since it was scheduled right before the lunch break.

Once the bell signaled the end of the lesson, I gathered my books and pencils and instead of following my classmates along the crowded corridor leading to the next lesson, I'd turn on my heels and head for the exit. Walking with a self-assured gait and eyes focused on my shoes, I continued my course having well plotted by journey earlier.

The wind on my face felt comforting after an endless morning strolling from one musty classroom to another. The buzzing chatter of students conversing about TV shows viewed the previous evening mixed with the laughter of young hearts living happy lives as children should—was quieted.

Clueless about the programs they were discussing, I had nothing to contribute to the conversation and certainly no sane reason to share their hearty laughs. Mine was a life of restriction and beatings, reprimands and loneliness, negligence and apathy.

Once outside I enjoyed the feeling of independence. Except for the vigilant presence of the sun, the embrace of a translucent blue sky, and the chirping echoes of shimmering blue-violet crows flapping their wings, no one was around to suffocate me or put an end to my living. The freedom of freedom was mesmerizing! I smiled.

I walked over to McDonald's, ordered a hamburger and a coke and gazed around at the giggling children seated with their parents. Their shirts were stained red with ketchup; their mouths were swollen with lunch. But I noticed how happy everyone looked—especially through the biased eyes familiar only with melancholy and misery.

Enjoying my time out far too much to be cautious about my escapades, my truancy gradually became more pronounced. One hour of freedom was no longer sufficient to calm a tortured soul begging for commiseration.

I started absenting myself from additional classes, heedful not to cut math because my grandmother Donna and my math teacher, Mr. Meyers, would often meet to discuss my progress.

In the evenings I returned to the invisible shackles and life within the four walls of my bedroom. My sister Cindy, undoubtedly the favorite daughter, was more fortunate. Two spankings from Uncle George at the age of four were the extent of her experience with physical abuse.

Seeing her howling and in pain, my mother intervened, claiming Cindy did not need corporal punishment because she was able to be reasoned with. "I can talk to Cindy," my mother said. "She is rational and understands what we expect of her. Margaret, on the other hand, needs firm discipline." Firm discipline translated to smarting wounds, sore bruises, physical violence and the mental torment of being grounded in one room.

Spurred by the awareness that my mother favored and protected Cindy and left me defenseless, at the mercy of Uncle George's authoritarian rampages, a tiny seed of jealousy was planted in my heart. Nurtured with constant reminders, it sprouted a little bit day by day until full-grown, it bore its noxious claws into my flesh.

We were in a sense 'Cain and Able' siblings. Cindy didn't like me in return for my not liking her—a relationship of reciprocity if nothing else. She felt I was a disruptive force, creating chaos and dissension in the house.

"Margaret, why can't you just learn to get along and do what Mom and Dad ask?" she'd say, her lips curling with disgust. "Life would be so much better and peaceful for us all. And you would be able to go out and have some fun like all the other kids instead of living all alone for months in your room."

I listened to what she said half-heartedly. It was nothing more than a string of words, pulling me further apart from her emotionally. How much credibility could the black sheep of the family give to the favorite daughter?

Cindy and I fought almost daily. The reasons made little if any difference. They served exclusively to get the tempers flaring. However, one day I discovered that Cindy, in cahoots with my mother, committed the most unpardonable crime—together they entered my room, uncovered my diary, and read page after page of my most intimate thoughts!

My privacy was invaded. My property was trespassed upon. I was furious. This time, instead of my innocence being stolen it was my dignity and respect. Peering into my thoughts and feelings was a serious violation, made sourer with Cindy's cruel teasing. The sin wasn't serious enough—she had to dangle the deed in front my face—flaunt her accomplishment. It was her way of 'confessing' the wrong she had done. But missing was even a faint morsel of remorse.

Though young girls, we tried to settle our differences through physical violence, the only way we knew. I lurched at her as she stood, brazenly showing off a spiteful sneer, stealing pleasure from my pain. Grabbing her hair, I yanked her to the ground. Caught off guard she lost her balance and fell, dragging me down on top of her. Legs and arms swinging and waving connected and separated, we tried to center our kicks and punches to any spot of the body that could possibly result in a hurt.

"You had no right to read my diary," I shouted, repeatedly slapping the side of her face with my open palm. In retaliation she threw me a swift kick that sent me skidding across the room. My bare legs burned from the friction of the linoleum on my skin. "You're bad," she screeched through clenched teeth. "That's why Dad beats you all the time. You deserve to be hit and slammed around!"

Breathless, she lost her grip on me. Pulling a clump of my hair from her mouth her attention was suddenly distracted. Taking full advantage of the 'blessing,' I rose to my feet, lunging my entire body at her. Once in a position of superiority, I pinned her arms to the floor. With a clumsy, jerky movement she kneed me in the *derrière*, sending me sprawling.

The echoes of shouts mixed with the thumping sounds of two unruly girls involved in a wrestling match brought my mother running to the room. Flinging open the door she caught sight of us red faced, tattered and disheveled.

"I'm not going to break this up," she said, almost enjoying the scene. "I'll let you battle it out until you kill each other!" Crossing her arms over her stomach she stood with a complacent look on her face as Cindy and I scrimmaged and fought like two rabid animals going for the jugular artery.

It never entered her mind to calm us down or at minimum put an end to the warfare. Instead, it seemed as if she obtained a sick pleasure from seeing her two children snarling and tearing each other apart.

Undoubtedly, this was a scenario more than suitable for one of the daytime talk shows designed to shock and awe an audience of both believers and skeptics. Since my dysfunctional life needed neither exaggeration nor enhancement to scandalize or repel, it gave me a different perspective about these often criticized TV hosts and their outrageous programs. Had I not personally witnessed and lived through the most outlandish episodes imaginable, practically on a daily basis, perhaps I, too, would have pronounced such shows 'staged.' However, since my drama was real, I questioned, "Why can't the others be, also?"

The shock factor arises not solely from the violent cursing scenes, but from the bitter reality that this brutish behavior and resulting lack of human respect and dignity is a despondent portrait of true life for some unfortunate individuals. It sends a message that sadly, there is no need to choreograph horror stories when they already exist in society.

Between my mother's chronic bouts of depression that triggered her to shut herself in her room without consenting to any contact or interaction with her family and Uncle George's out-of-control alcoholism, life had crossed the line linking dysfunctional with despicably toxic.

By this time my parents no longer shared a room, and Uncle George was relegated to the couch. Family dinners were cancelled, forcing us to fend for ourselves if we didn't want to starve to death. My mother was working and exhausted from her melancholy, erratic moods wings. Simultaneously, Uncle George stumbled in every evening around eight, reeking of liquor, uttering incomprehensible, slurred words.

On one occasion he flung open the door so swiftly the door knob bashed an indentation in the wall. Tiny splinters of paint and plaster rained on the green shag carpet. Uncle George was so intoxicated he had to lean against the wall to keep from falling face down.

Grumbling, he frisked his own pocket with his free hand. Rocking back and forth on unsteady feet, he pulled out his packet of Marlboros, dropping several coins. He shook the pack and with his yellow-stained front teeth extracted a cigarette. A hacking cough and poor coordination brought it down on the carpet.

Uncle George grunted en route to retrieving it. A trembling hand reinserted the cigarette between his lips while the other one searched his coat pocket for the lighter. He took a few wobbly steps before trying to light the cigarette. After two flicks the bright yellow flame stood at attention. I smelled the lighter fluid. Malodorous as it was, the stink was kinder to my nostrils than Uncle George's nauseating breath.

Raising the flame to the cigarette, he inhaled. It didn't light. Repeating the procedure he again inhaled, once ... twice ... three times. Again, the cigarette did not light. Uncle George's face was contorted and beet red. Too drunk to realize the reason for his failure, he tried over and over without success.

Frustrated, he opened his mouth to release a curse, dropping the cigarette on the floor. Seated on the couch, I observed his almost irrational annoyance and the beginnings of a wild tantrum.

Uncle George was far too alcohol saturated to realize he was trying to light the filter end of the cigarette, and petrified, I now realized there was a bigger picture to all this nightmarish behavior. Even if I was still ill-equipped to 'see' it all, I knew something was seriously wrong.

Unaware the school principle had called Uncle George to report I had cut a class, I got up from the dining room chair and headed for the kitchen. He was furious and I feared a nasty confrontation.

When Uncle George noticed my exit, he first followed me with his eyes, then with slowed reflexes staggered after me. His breathing was heavy, almost panting. I was cornered. Grabbing my waist-length hair he twisted it tightly to get a better grip. Treating it as a chord he dragged me first across the kitchen then swung me around the room. Caught off guard by this unannounced punishment alteration from belt to bare hands, I lost my balance, crashing down with a thump.

There was no pity—no compassion. The dragging continued. The pulling worsened. Terrified by the strength of sheer madness, I felt clumps of hair being wrenched from my scalp. My head burned—the pain was throbbing—excruciating, in competition only with a paralyzing fear. I was unarmed and standing at the front in the direct line of enemy fire!

When my spin on the linoleum floor slowed a bit, Uncle George leaned over to swat me across the face. His ring caught the edge of my lower lip, slicing it wide open. Blood splattered like a faucet—dripping down my neck, eventually forming a small *Rorschach* ink blot type stain on my shirt, giving insight into the mind of insanity.

Powered by rage, his hand went farther. Tightening into a fist, it slammed into my nose—another spurt of blood. Panic-stricken, I touched my face to see if I still had teeth and noticed my nose was swollen. Shaking like a half-crumpled, semi-parched autumn leaf caught in its final tropical storm, I thought it was my end. The punishment was so different from the ritualistic belt lashings that were such a familiar part of my life. This was a merciless assault!

"Uncle George is going to kill me," I whispered to myself as my mother walked into the kitchen. Without taking her eyes off me, without the faintest trace of compassion on her hardened face, and without coming over to assist or console me she said, "George, what is going on?"

"It—it was an accident," Uncle George stammered. "I—I didn't mean to hit her like that. My ring caught her l-lip and cut it open. You know she—she cut class again. The principal called me to gi-give me the news. He—he was very upset. She—she has to learn. She has to—to be punished. This is the on-only language she understands—but-but-it-was an accident. I—I didn't mean to do this!"

During his stuttering tirade, I lifted myself up and ran to my room. Climbing up the staircase was not easy. My legs felt heavy, almost numb. I was dizzy from the blood loss and dazed from the unimaginable violence.

Certain my best tactic was to get as far away as possible from them, I went to my room, slammed the door shut and curled myself up in a doughnut, hurriedly tugging the covers over my head with whatever strength I had left in my aching arms.

Uncle George's screams and stammering lies were still audible. My mother became upset with his drunken rage and ranted back. I despised the very sound of their voices. I just couldn't get their words out of my mind no matter how hard I tried—no matter how loudly I played my radio.

The echoes bounced from one side of my head to the other—trapped inside with no way out, like a handful of wasps locked in a cage trying to sting their way to freedom. They got louder and louder—piercing my ear drums. I struggled to withdraw into myself—to lose myself in my own fantasy. But the echoes persisted—haunting me—menacing me, bullying me.

Filled with hate, I pulled the pillow over my ears—it was my last attempt to silence the horror. "I wish they were dead," I screamed into the pillow. "I wish they were dead!"

A restless night of throbbing pain, quivering sobs and an unknown terror that kept me sleepless and ever conscious of my misery drenched my pajamas and bed sheets with an icy sweat.

The following morning, stiff, bleary-eyed and visibly swollen and bruised I went to school. The vice principal as well as my teachers noticed my debilitated state. They were aware of the repeated physical and emotional abuse of which I was a habitual victim—without reprieve.

However, in the early 80s there was not much legal recourse available, and non-parental authority figures thought it best not to address the issues of 'alleged' abuse for fear of aggravating the situation for the child involved. Instead, the situation was wound up in silence and denial forcing children to accept the beatings and emotional torture without assistance, medication or support. They were threatened to keep quiet or face additional punishment. The reputation of the family was at stake. But who worried about the children?

Silence serves only to encourage the villains, until accountability and responsibility liberates some of the victims from the dangerous criminal actions that endanger their lives as well as their minds—and not without deep life-long scars.

Uncle George's rampage gave me a new awareness. It was a turning-point moment, a life-altering experience that sent me down a very new and challenging path.

Emotionally disassociated from my family at thirteen years of age, I realized I had to continue alone or succumb—a victim of parental criminal folly. I opted for survival realizing I had to be prepared and armed for the battle of my life.

Chapter 4

The Second Trial:
Life is Full of Suffering

"My own utterance I will not restrain;
I will speak in the anguish of my spirit;
I will complain in the bitterness of my soul."
—Job 7:11

At first the hatred in my heart was so intense it consumed every waking thought. Then it began to spiral as the days passed, eventually trespassing beyond, invading my dreams like an ungovernable malignancy with a poison impossible to cure.

Bitter and brimming over with rancor, I felt the heat of loathing rush through me, leaving in its wake a trail of confusion, misery and hopelessness. The two years I had spent on restriction, together with the forfeited football games and dances as well as the total cut-off from life outside of school left me with no outlet to cool the burning within. I had no deliverance from the beatings, no pause from my parents' wild mood swings jumping between anger and apathy.

My one reprieve from the torment was the exhilaration of my 'restriction escape.' I was getting out—but best of all I was deliberately defying Uncle George.

Looking back, I cannot imagine how at fourteen years of age I was able to successfully sneak out from my bedroom window on the second floor without slipping and breaking my neck.

Apparently, I had a strategy. Crawling out the window one leg at a time and careful not to lose my balance, I'd settle my *derrière* on the red tile roof. Although it slopped dangerously, without a moments hesitation, I'd propel myself forward pushing with the palms of my hands until I slid to the edge.

Once at the edge of the roof, I'd hesitate just long enough to take a deep breath and shut my eyes. Seconds later I'd jump to the ground, landing in the softness of the lush blades of grass. Thankfully, they served as a safety net—buffering the impact, thus protecting me from injury.

Perhaps the thought of a few hours away from the absurd sprees of violence made the risk of getting caught and whipped or seriously hurt, worthwhile. Or maybe with the thought of actually being able to have fun like all the other kids my age, I just never really considered the consequences.

Once I was on the ground, I swung my right hand around and dusted off my *derrière*. I ran down the street to meet my best friend, Stephanie, and her mother who were waiting for me.

Stephanie, who had befriended me since seventh grade, was a prototype of the typical California girl. Silky, waist-length blond hair, a huge pair of dazzling blue eyes, and a down-to-earth, vivacious, outgoing personality enhanced the natural beauty of her fourteen years.

Unlike most of my other friends, she was neither intimidated nor afraid to visit my house during the rare and far in between intervals in which Uncle George issued a reprieve from restriction. Furthermore, unlike some others, she was not forbidden from crossing the threshold at my entry door, even if many of the 'events' of my tormented life were pretty much known among my teachers, friends, and their parents.

When Stephanie did come, she'd establish immediate eye contact with Uncle George. Never flinching a moment, she'd address him with the same courtesy and respect she would any other adult.

Surprisingly, Uncle George took a liking to her. In return for her kindness he would engage her in conversation, actually enjoying her company. Consequently, Stephanie was the only friend he and my mother actually approved of.

Stephanie's mother, who was unaware of my 'sneaking out' escape routine, would accompany us with her car since as high school freshmen we were not yet qualified to apply for a driver's license.

Like a seasoned 'criminal' intent on plotting each prison break with the precision and accuracy of a clock maker, to prevent any and all oversights that could eventually lead to capture, I studied my options carefully. Realizing sliding down the tile roof was a game of chance, whereas climbing up required a strength and skill I did not have, I knew I would have to find a diverse return strategy.

After much thought I decided to leave the dining room window on the ground floor open, just wide enough for me to pass through with ease. No one would notice, since the family no longer gathered around the table for meals. But more importantly, I would be able to easily slip back in without creating a ruckus or risk killing myself.

For quite some time I was privileged. My 'escape smarts' and a bit of good luck kept me a smiling participant at all football games and school dances even if, officially, I was still on restriction.

However, as most gamblers eventually learn, the life-expectancy of luck is unpredictably short—it never springs eternal. Nonetheless, it does run dry, often without warning and in the least opportune moment.

I soon learned this important lesson when towards the end of freshman year fortune betrayed me through Janie's anger. A tall, strapping girl almost double my size, Janie enjoyed a certain popularity among her own group of friends. Upset with me one evening after a football game, she advanced towards me following a West Side Story strategy backed by her friends. Post game intimidation was her tactic.

Initially out-numbered, soon several other kids headed by Stephanie came to my rescue. However, the skirmish was a one on one conflict exclusively between Janie and me.

Fearless and self-assured, she stepped ahead of her 'band' right under the bleachers and inched towards me with strong determined steps. The length of her legs encouraged a wide, sturdy gait that made her look even more empowering.

Brazen and confident, she pounced ready for her attack. Standing no higher than her shoulders, I locked my arms around her waist. With one swift movement, I lifted her off her feet and threw her four or five feet, actually injuring myself. Stunned, she fell to the ground with a vibrating thud, staring at me in disbelief.

One of her male friends came to her defense. He approached, arms outstretched ready to seek revenge. "Why did you do that to Janie?" he snorted. Angered, I pushed and shoved him before he could strike me. Losing his footing he stumbled, fell back and landed with his *derrière* on the ground, mortified that a girl more than half his size had knocked him down.

For a brief moment, the deafening silence of shock prevailed—interrupted only by the sudden animated cheers and comments of the other kids who had witnessed my feats of inexplicable strength!

How could this have been possible? I questioned in the quiet of my mind. *Both Janie and her friend are almost double my size—and he's a guy!*

Awed by the display of such exceptional power, I remained alone with my thoughts, justifying my actions as self-defense since my opponents were indisputably the aggressors.

By nature I did not believe physical violence was a justifiable way to resolve issues and except for my angry wrestling matches with Cindy, I had never raised a hand to another child.

Horrified, I recognized the onset of a disturbing violent streak developing within. Suddenly, perhaps triggered by the anger seeded with parental rejection and abuse, it manifested itself in my almost surreal physical strength. It seemed as if all the pain and humiliation endured at home gave life to a steroidal rage, fueling me with an overdose of premium adrenaline energy.

That evening Janie's mother phoned my mom. "Margaret hit Janie in the bleachers after the football game today," she said, bluntly opening the conversation. "She picked her up, then slammed her down, hurting her. The other kids said she was like a mad demon, going after Janie for no reason, then shoving and attacking another boy who came to her rescue! Vivian—this is unacceptable behavior for a young girl—it's outrageous. You have to put an end to it before she seriously injures another child."

Janie's mother had sealed my fate. My parents were now fully aware I had broken restriction and snuck out to attend a football game. They also realized I had made a mockery of Uncle George's punishment!

When delivered the news of my insubordination, Uncle George stammered through pursed lips, "Margaret, you're incorrigible—we can no longer control you! I don't know what else to do."

"George," my mom chimed in, "I think Margaret has the same awful illness my mother has. She must have inherited the depression. She's mentally ill—that's the problem. That's why she acts the way she does."

Nothing was resolved with my mother's 'diagnosis,' but as a course of treatment my restriction was prolonged. The added sentence neither intimidated me nor deterred my escapes. Keeping my 'Incorrigible' reputation in tact, I continued my roof sliding, window climbing tactics to attend football games and dances. After all, it was just clean fun teens have a right to enjoy.

Immunity had affected him. I no longer feared Uncle George and my mother. There was nothing they could say or do that would change my mind about how I felt—I continued to loathe them both! It was that pure and equally as simple.

Sporadically, luck would double cross me, and I'd get caught at my own game. Faced with Uncle George's harsh recriminations and repeated belt lashings, I started to rebel. His drinking worsened. I could smell the liquor on his breath as soon as he came through the door—even before he opened his mouth to yell at me.

Loud screeching insults ensued as I stood up to him and his drunken rants. "I can't stand you—I can't stand it here anymore," I shouted. "I don't want to spend my life shut in my bedroom without ever going out to games and dances or seeing my friends. No other kid gets this kind of punishment. I'm on restriction over two years—I've had enough!"

Trumping a slap to the face or a nasty rebuttal with slurred admonishments, I threw up my arms and ran out of the room, leaving his outrageous bellowing echoes exclusively for his own ears.

"Mom," I said, gathering my wits, "can I spend the weekend at Stephanie's house? She asked if I could come."

"Well, what about her mother—did she tell you to come?"

"Mrs. Cronin is very shy," I responded, "but she said it is OK."

Actually, Stephanie ruled the house. Playing a major role, she had a big influence in the upbringing of her younger siblings. Usually, their mother listened to her daughters' requests.

Mrs. Cronin was a timid, petite woman, often manipulated by her daughter. When Stephanie wanted me to come—I came. Soon learning the full intensity of my family history, she was horrified by the physical abuse and believed she could convince her mother to let me move in on a permanent basis.

However, the suggestion was not well received. Mrs. Cronin assumed her responsibility as an adult in the household and firmly denied her daughter's request.

"Stephanie," she said, "we cannot involve ourselves in this situation. From what I understand this family needs professional help. There are serious issues— perhaps more than you or I know. I agree—it sounds as if something is very wrong, and I feel sorry for Margaret, but we are not in a position to step in and pull her away from her parents."

"Mom," Stephanie said, "can I at least invite her to come and stay for short visits?"

Delighted to receive a nod of approval from her mother, Stephanie believed she had made some progress in trying to make my life easier. Thanks to her kindness, I started spending weekends at the Cronins' to escape the folly at my own house. Life was so different—it was so nurturing at Stephanie's that once I took advantage of their generosity and stretched my visit to last a week.

Mr. Cronin was a charming gentleman who doted on Stephanie, often spoiling her with his exaggerated attentions. Kind and generous, he welcomed me with a bright smile, treating me as one of the family. I felt liked and accepted for the first time in my life. It was such a monumental change from my own family and peers.

As early as junior high, I was pretty popular even though the other kids knew something was not quite right. Often commenting about my roof sliding escapades to attend dances and football games they'd question, "Why don't your parents allow you to go out?"

Concealing my misery behind a lighthearted personality, I was forever cracking jokes, projecting my sense of humor and making the kids laugh with my comedy-like antics.

In fact, years earlier I had been voted 'class clown;' an award denied by the vice principal because as he put it, "It will encourage your vibrant and disruptive conduct." Then addressing the class he repeated, "I know you all voted Margaret as the class clown, but giving her this award would mean we condone her unruly and disturbing behavior—and we cannot." With this consideration rendered public, the other children understood something was not quite right. Consequently, I paid the price.

Therefore, gaining the approval of the Cronin family was a new experience, one I actually enjoyed. Not only did I receive the joy of their warmth and hospitality, but I learned how valuable a loving, supportive and fostering family can be.

Whenever warfare broke out at my house, I'd escape to Stephanie's for a bit of peace and quiet. 'Incorrigible' as my parents said I was, they soon discovered it was impossible to lock me in the house.

One of our other neighbors was a girl named Lee whose mother was a psychiatrist and very much aware of my family situation. Empathetic and kind, Lee and her mother always welcomed me into their home whenever I was in distress.

No longer permitted to escape to Stephanie's house, I'd seek solace from my anguish and the bitter bickering at Lee's. Of course, Lee's mom interrogated me to better understand why I was so distraught and frequently 'on the run' from my own house.

I told her of the humiliating belt lashings, offensive shouting matches, Uncle George's out-of-control drinking, my mother's chronic debilitating depression and my two-year and continuing restriction in my bedroom.

The following morning, at her insistence, I accompanied the doctor to work while she explored some different options that would remove me from my toxic surroundings and allow me to get the assistance she felt I needed.

Deciding on the JCRP, the Juvenile Crisis Resolution Program, which removes children from dysfunctional, abusive families, she followed the legal process, declared me a runaway and engaged a police officer to pick me up.

According to legal protocol, I was taken to the station, booked as a runaway and then driven home where I waited in the car while the law enforcement officer went inside to speak with Uncle George regarding my return to the family.

Asked if I would be welcomed back into the house, Uncle George said, "I don't want Margaret living here with us any longer. She is mentally ill and needs treatment."

Seated in the rear of the police vehicle, scared by the uncertainty of my future, I felt the heat of anxiety creep up behind my neck. Confused, I could not respond to my own question—did I want to go home or to jail?

Upon receiving Uncle George's refusal I was taken to Juvenile Hall, fingerprinted and officially booked as a runaway. I stayed there for forty-eight hours before being released to the Juvenile Crisis Resolution Program.

Mr. Qubicz presented himself on my behalf and was placed in my care.

Juvenile Hall had been a terrifying, traumatic experience. Thrown together with teen-age gang members and other violent types who had been convicted of serious crimes, I sat in my loneliness. *What happened to me? How could my life have taken such a nasty turn? Why did my life become such a nightmare?*

Once in the JCRP, I was enrolled in the temporary foster care program. This meant I would be sent to live with different families for brief periods of time until my own situation was rehabbed or I turned sixteen years of age, and as a ward of the state would be in a position to live unsupervised, financially providing for my own upkeep.

The County assigned me a counselor, Bill Qubicz, a slender man of short stature with a kind, tender heart. Like Uncle George, his visually challenged eyes were narrowly set behind dark-rimmed coke bottle glasses.

Mr. Qubicz was young and dressed well, building his wardrobe from eighties fashion trends. Janet, his tall, thin, striking, soft-spoken partner was also a full time mental health counselor for teen-agers and active in helping kids get the assistance they needed. Both professionals were dedicated advocates, empathetic and gracious in my regard.

They intervened, setting up several meetings with my parents to isolate and define the issues that needed quick attention, devise a solution and decide which program would be most beneficial for my situation and personality.

After a careful evaluation I was placed with a foster family, and once a week Bill would visit, pick me up and accompany me to his office for a meeting with my parents. This program was structured on brevity and frequent connections for a smooth re-insertion from the host parents to the biological family.

Initially, I was placed in a shelter for battered and abused children, Hillcrest Receiving Home in downtown San Diego, until a foster family was found to accommodate my needs. It seemed as if I was asked and answered an endless barrage of questions about my family life, school and health.

Hillcrest was situated high on a hill, overlooking the San Diego Freeway's major I-Five beltway. Looking like an austere stereotyped mental facility/prison, it had an unkempt, grassy soccer field behind the main entrance—the only sign of normalcy.

A one-level sprawling, massive brick structure, the home was set on several acres of land. Heavily barred, the windows faced the seven-foot chain link fence that seemed to hug the perimeters of the property, threatening an escape-free environment for the children residing behind the metal barrier.

Though intentioned as a rehab for disturbed teens, Hillcrests 'guests' were a devastating array of mistreated and severely abused infants, toddlers and children.

Observing my fellow-inmates brought into the light an unbelievable reality of horrendous crimes committed against innocent, defenseless individuals. Shocked by the appalling condition of these children, I was swept into an overwhelming state of depression.

Infants as young as six months old lay immobile in scratched and dented cribs like tattered rag dolls waiting to be sewn back together again. Their tiny, frail bodies, burned and badly bruised, were rigid and contorted in agony.

Toddler faces already stamped with the pain and frustration symbolizing a lifetime of hard living, gazed at me as I bent over to pat their bowed heads. Even a gentle caress was received with a grimace and withdrawal—obviously interpreted as a menacing threat of more whippings and sexual molestation. Fear and anguish clouded the room like the dense layer of smog often entombing Los Angeles.

Placed among the little ones despite my age, I saw hundreds of barely breathing carcasses, limp feeble bodies that had experienced every form and intensity of violence and aggression but the actual deathblow.

Children barely older than toddlers were hurried inside, swaddled in blood-stained sheets and towels—their faint whimpers, the only sign of life.

Many three, four and five-year-olds had suffered severe consequences from repeated bouts of maltreatment. Not yet weaned from their diapers, they were still unable to walk.

Viewing the horrors of serious negligence and criminal misdeeds, I felt misplaced at Hillcrest. How sad—abused and molested myself, I lost all measure of the wrong to me committed—and all because I had seen the suffering faces and wounded, badly scarred bodies of exaggerated brutality. However, this should not have defined my life as an existence within the guideline of normal acceptable behavior.

I actually felt privileged. "I guess my life is not so bad," I whispered to myself, "especially in comparison to the hell these babies and children have been through."

It's amazing how unimportant belt lashings, sexual molestation, beatings and endless restriction can seem in just a few short days. It's incredible how easy it is to warp the mind and perspective of a young impressionable teen.

Classes at Hillcrest Receiving Home were a daily ritual. About twenty kids in all, we sat from nine until around five learning math, history, English, science and geography. However, too deep into my depression, I soon began withdrawing from the other children and slipping off to be with my despondent thoughts.

Walking outside, I'd feel almost listless, dragging my feet until I reached the vacant soccer field. Throwing myself down on the dried brown patches of grass, often trampled on by running soccer players competing for a goal, I'd sit and stare into space for endless periods of time.

Disheartened, I'd switch my focused gaze at the highway which was in clear view from the soccer field. Knowing my mother traveled on the freeway en route to work each day, I'd sit practically immobile, turning my neck from side to side, following each speeding car with my eyes in a desperate attempt to spot my mother's Honda.

After awhile my absence from class and resulting presence on the soccer field became obvious to the therapists and teachers. They soon realized, in tears, I was searching for my mother.

Mr. Qubicz was attentive, stopping by for a visit on a weekly basis. "Margaret," he'd say, patting me on the head, "I know you're not very happy here. You don't really belong here and I'm working very hard to get you out. We'll soon find a foster family for you so you can leave Hillcrest."

A qualified professional, Mr. Qubicz recognized my worsening bouts of depression, realizing I was not gaining any benefits from my tenure at the receiving home. If anything, the devastating environment was aggravating the effects of my dysfunctional upbringing.

To rectify the situation he arranged a counseling session with my parents which surprisingly went quite well. The general belief was that in separating me from my family both parties would have time to mentally and emotionally regroup before we reunited again.

During the meeting Mr. Qubicz addressed Uncle George, "I think Margaret's condition here at Hillcrest is deteriorating," he said. "Her depression has become more pronounced; therefore, I do not feel this is the right path to follow. I believe she would do better if you had a family counselor come to your home and work with you as a family."

Uncle George and my mother, self-diagnosing me as mentally ill, were dubious of the validity of Mr. Qubicz's recommendation.

The possibility of returning home initially uplifted my mood. Just to remove myself from the Hillcrest 'horrors' was already a depression 'quasher,' even if of temporary duration.

Oddly, despite the negligence and emotional coolness, I longed to be with my mother. I guess the mother-child bond survives even the most outlandish displays of indifference, abandon and neglect. Somehow it is formed in the womb during the nine months of pregnancy and not easily ruptured—at least in my case. I missed her during my stay at Hillcrest and yearned to be back in my own home.

The desolation and human suffering witnessed during those few weeks was traumatizing for a young teen. Shocked and dismayed by the realization of the awful crimes committed against even infants, I withdrew, eventually burying myself in a more tangled web of depression. However, the possibility of leaving did put a smile on my face—albeit, a faint flickering one.

The new found family serenity lasted for about two weeks. I returned to my high school and friends. The restriction was lifted and the 'privilege' to attend football games and dances was given as an entitlement.

Unfortunately, heavily influenced by my Hillcrest experience, my grades took a sharp dive from As and Bs to barely passing Ds. When Uncle George read my report card, he said, "Margaret, this is awful—you barely passed. Too much going out with your friends, I guess, doesn't give you time to study. Well, I see I'll have to fix that problem. Until you bring me As and Bs, you're back on restriction. Do you understand?"

With my nod of approval, I lied. I could neither accept nor understand anything about the validity of abuse.

Right before my sophomore year, I met a group of sixteen to eighteen-year-old punk rockers who seemed to have a free and irresponsible life that caught my fancy. Confrontational, anti-establishment and rebellious, their 'regardless of consequences' way of behaving tempted me. No longer accepting my abusive lifestyle, the idea of not having anyone to order me around, beat me or force me into restriction was too appealing to resist. I hung around awhile trying to better understand 'who they were' and how they spent their days.

Homeless, most of them carried their meager belongs in backpacks and moved from street to street setting up a refuge for the night.

Dressed in black clothing with long knee length silver chains dangling from a hip-hugger pant loop, they had numerous visible skin piercings and colorful enigmatic tattoos. A central bush of erect, bristle-like spiked hair, tinted in various shades of green, purple, red or yellow, according to personal preference, enhanced semi-shaven heads. Dark bright make-up extravagantly applied to their faces in exaggerated patterns completed the look.

If there was any rhyme or reason to the punk rockers' physical appearance and fashion selections, it was unknown to me. It was all in the 'do it yourself' mindset and philosophy so openly and brazenly represented.

Attracted to this group, I started to hang around with them after school whenever I could slide down the roof and escape restriction. One of the kids took a look at my waist length hair. "Margaret," he said, tugging on my hair, "this has to go. Don't worry, I'll do it for you."

Ten minutes later my head was a smooth bald palate except for a long ultra-skinny tail swinging from the nape of my neck! Strewn about the floor were mounds of my shorn locks.

When I returned home my mother was appalled. "Margaret, what have you done?" she shouted, red-faced and breathless. "When your dad sees this he'll beat you to your death. I won't have this—this is mortifying. I cannot be seen anywhere with you in that condition. I think you'd better find another place to live."

Even my friend Stephanie and her family were mortified and horrified by my new hairdo and what it represented.

Thankfully, one of the punk kids, my friend Lee, had use of a one bedroom apartment located near the railroad tracks in an impoverished part of the city. It was dilapidated and dingy, a ramshackle hovel with cracks, chipped paint and dark mold stains blazing a trail along the walls.

I crammed in with Lee, another girl and two boys, sleeping on a cold, badly soiled linoleum floor that smelled and looked like it had not been tended to in years. The permeating aroma of an unkempt house mixed with the sweaty, un-bathed bodies of a group of teenagers had to be nauseating. However, the ruthlessness and sheer thrill of the unconventional attitude made it a non-issue.

Since survival depends not only on a roof covering but on nourishment, the kids would break into their parents' homes to steal money and jewelry with which to buy food.

When we went to my house all we found was a piece of cheap jewelry worth about ten dollars that belonged to my mother. However, every little bit helped when dirt poor; therefore, satisfied, we moved on to hit and ransack another house.

Although the punk rock movement was popular at the time, I took it to the extreme—actually thinking or deluding myself into believing I could escape my dysfunctional world by joining this seemingly carefree environment. But happiness and peace of mind would never be found on the streets. Happiness was more than a semi-shaved head, wildly dyed hair, baggy black pants, chains, punk rock music, non-conventional commune style living, stealing for food for survival, and a 'don't care do your own thing attitude.'

Truant from school, we just hung out around the tracks—five lost, unruly teens in rebellion, desperately searching though clueless about what we were looking for. Perhaps running away from, more than towards the reality of who we were!

Though I did not indulge in drinking, I would sit on the porch of the liquor store, idle while the others drank. Then one day while I waited for my friends to come out with their drinks, a gentleman pulled up in a fancy luxury car. Stopping short in front of me, he opened the door and walked right up to me, saying, "You know, you have such a beautiful face—why would you shave your head and do this to yourself?"

Speechless, I gaped at him, unwillingly dropping my lower jaw. He was an attractive, well dressed man either in his late thirties or early forties. Though his dark eyes were questioning, his smile was warm, almost caring. He looked at my white T-shirt, black saggy pants complete with the status symbol silver chain and just shook his well coiffed head of dark hair.

Whether he was a concerned individual perhaps with a son or daughter my age or an angel sent from heaven, I didn't know at the time. But he seemed to care like no one else ever did. And his few kind words gave me my first compliment. More importantly, they convinced me life on the streets was not the path to happiness—it was time to return home.

While I was living on the streets, unknown to me, Uncle George discovered the brake lines on his Pinto had been cut. Believing I wanted him dead, the blame was put on my shoulders until the real culprit was found many years thereafter—a fellow colleague. I guess I was not the only one who despised Uncle George!

However, though I was not involved, when I did learn of the incident I had hoped he would have driven himself to death down some fast highway lane; even if as a prime suspect with a reasonable motive, I probably would have been arrested and charged with homicide.

Meanwhile, my parents hoped my two-week mutinous experience 'on the streets' would be so shocking and overwhelming as to actually teach me a lesson.

When I returned home, there was no opposition either from Uncle George or my mother. My reentry and re-insertion in the family was relatively non-eventful.

All the wiser for my punk interlude, I realized this was neither where I should be nor where I wanted to be. It was lifestyle, albeit free and unstructured, a bit too self-deprecatory and insignificant. There was no destination—only a jumbled mess of obstructed paths and confusing detours, leading either nowhere or to a dead-end cul-de-sac where no human being cares to go.

Lee had also returned home to her family, and my hair started to grow back. About a week later, she gave me some distressing news which had spread throughout the school. Since this was the era of rock punk mania, all the kids followed the different groups and took an interest in the happenings.

One of the older boys and his brother, two hard-core rock *punkers* who were living with us in the apartment got a buzz jumping on the tracks in front of an incoming train, then running to the other side just seconds before the cars would cross. Believing they were invincible they'd take outlandish risks for a quick thrill.

Their indomitable approach to danger soon defeated them. During one of their irrational duels against fate, they tripped over the tracks and both were gruesomely decapitated. Though I never participated in this activity, I just stood around and watched with Lee.

For a very brief interlude until the fate she and Uncle George had been plotting for me would come to be, my mother allowed visits with friends and participation in some after school activities—privileges that lasted just a few weeks.

Outgoing and friendly, I easily won the approval of other kids. Invitations came for parties and weekends. Visiting another friend, Monica, with Stephanie one afternoon, my mother dropped by unexpectedly to pick me up on her way home from work.

She seemed more withdrawn than usual, rarely making eye contact. I noticed her hands trembled slightly and a sudden stream of tears began swimming down her cheeks. Quiet, I waited for her to speak though I felt my pulse quickening.

Monica and Stephanie stood near, hardly daring to breathe. There was a feeling of tense uncertainty—like something was about to happen—and I was not the only one who felt it.

After blowing her nose, my mother cleared her throat. "Margaret," she said, turning her puffed, bloodshot eyes on me, "we have found a new home for you. You will be going away for two weeks."

"Where am I going?" I asked, puzzled. I had tried very hard to behave myself since my return and didn't understand this sudden decision to send me away again.

"You're going to South Wood Mental Health Facility," she responded, "for a two week evaluation. Your dad and I think it's a good idea considering your past behavior."

Stephanie and Monica turned to look at me. I could see their eyes mist with tears. "Why?" I asked, sobbing. "Please don't send me there, Mom," I continued, refusing to wait for a response I was certain I would not get. "I don't belong in a mental health facility. I don't want to go there—don't make me."

I continued my begging and pleading with her in the car all the way back to the house. She drove around a couple of times trying to calm me down explaining, "It's only for a couple of weeks and then you'll be back home."

I found no comfort in her 'reassurances.' Somehow, I couldn't find it in my heart to trust her. Something was not right!

When we stepped out of the Honda, I was confronted by the mental health facility people who had jumped out from the van as soon as we pulled into the driveway.

Disturbed by the underhanded turn of events, I soon realized it was all pre-orchestrated by Uncle George and my mom. Therefore, as soon as we arrived, they were ready and waiting to immediately accompany me to Southwood Mental Health Facility in Chula Vista on the Mexican border.

They had set it all up behind my back! This was why they permitted me to come back home after my episode on the streets and why my mom came to Monica's to drive me home and give me the news.

I was driven to Chula Vista, crying all the way. After a two hour drive, the van stopped in front of a massive chain link fence topped with about a foot of rusting, tangled barbed-wire. The driver exited and went to the speaker phone. A few seconds later the gate opened.

I held my breath as we drove up to the one story brick building. It was set on several acres of well-landscaped land with a surprising abundance of trees. Yet, despite the flourishing verdant back drop, I noticed the building was just as gigantic and equally as hideous as Hillcrest. However, this time I was not shut in a receiving home—but 'imprisoned' in a mental health facility!

Inside South Wood looked like a typical hospital—nondescript, impressionably antiseptic and relatively silent. The pungent odor of a heavy sterilizing disinfectant burned my nostrils. Kicking and screaming, I felt my hands being roughly pulled together. A big burly attendant dragged me to a room. He smelled of body oder and tobacco, and his hands were cold and calloused.

"I don't want to be here," I shouted hysterically. "Get me out of here! I don't belong here! I'm not crazy."

I tried to stick my foot out the front door which was interpreted as a rebellious gesture. "You'll be allowed to go home, Margaret, after two weeks if we don't find any signs of mental illness," I was told. Believing their words, I was shut down into silence and resignation.

Once I was settled in and accepting of my fate, I realized the facility was well run and staffed with competent, compassionate individuals who treated me with kindness and understanding.

I was placed in a wing reserved exclusively for teenagers whose parents or insurance policies had paid to have them committed. I was scheduled for a two-week evaluation, since previously labeled 'incorrigible' by my mother and Uncle George who were in total accord about my 'inherited mental illness.'

After a series of tests I had many one-on-one dialogues with my psychiatrist, a balding, middle-aged white-haired man with a distinctive receding hairline. Dr. Marsh wore gold-rimmed glasses and was always exceptionally well-groomed, including manicured nails and a musky scent of aftershave, giving the impression of a successful professional.

Dr. Marsh's face was pleasant and jovial, inspiring trust, unlike some of the stereotype Hollywood psychiatrists, often cast as eccentric and somewhat unstable with respect to society's definition of normalcy.

My room resembled an undecorated college dorm with white walls and linoleum. I had a roommate, a sixteen-year-old Moslem Iranian girl who suffered from severe anorexia. Sadly, she was at the point of refusing all food. Her parents knew the sickness was endangering her life and sought immediate professional treatment at South Wood.

I was explained the dangers of this debilitating illness that afflicts young people—girls more than boys. It was all new to me, but I listened attentively. It sounded ruthless and I was reassured that although it could be fatal, it was curable with a quick diagnosis as soon as symptoms of excessive weight loss and radical food refusal appeared and appropriate treatment was administered.

The poor girl was listless. She seemed on the brink of death. There was no life in her eyes, and her personality was as flat as a postmortem EKG—such a contrast to my dynamic nature. However, one afternoon after returning to my room from a family session I found her sprawled in a pool of blood in the restroom we shared. She had unsuccessfully tried to commit suicide by slitting her wrists.

My encounter with the young anorexic brought me to the realization that despite all my suffering and tribulations, I was not a person who would ever try to end my life. Instead, I was strong-willed and determined to fight my demons head on, never accepting anything less than triumph as an end result.

My evaluation included observations and blood work, as well as numerous brain scans both in a waking and sleep state because I had spoken of my haunted house experiences and terrifying nightmares. Dr. Marsh had explained to me reasons for my nightmares. "Your subconscious is orchestrating these nightmares about your house," he said, "as a means of helping you deal with the situation head on!"

I didn't give his words much credibility, holding firm to my theory that the house was haunted and my family was possessed by evil spirits.

At the conclusion of the two-week period, Dr. Marsh summoned my parents and Cindy for a conference.

"I am happy to tell you that after a complete evaluation, we have found there is nothing clinically wrong with Margaret," he said, looking them directly in the eyes. It is our opinion that her depression stems from her unhealthy home environment. Ethically, we can no longer keep her here at South Wood. We are dismissing her to your care."

"There is definitely something wrong with her," Uncle George shouted, rising to his feet. Beet red, his face was contorted in the grimace of an irrational man.

"You absolutely have to keep her here! I don't think you have done enough testing to find out what's wrong with her. And until you do, I want her to remain here and not at home."

What Uncle George refused to accept was the truth—he was a vital part of my problem! Informed of this possibility, he protested angrily. "I cannot and will not deal with the likes of her at home!"

Much as Dr. Marsh was a congenial, agreeable gentleman with the gentle manner of a diplomat, his antipathy for my parents was more than obvious. His jaw tightened and I could see he was grinding his teeth. If he was uncertain before, he now had the confirmation of who and what, were responsible for my depression. It was obvious—Uncle George and my mother were not only the root of my emotional issues, but the poison triggering my rebellious behavior.

"Well, Margaret," Dr. Marsh said, clearing his throat, "there isn't any medication we can prescribe to help you with your problems. What I can do is find you a nice foster family who will look after you. In the meantime we will keep you with us at South Wood."

After my roommate was discharged, I remained in the mental health facility in a private room for four months—until Uncle George's insurance stopped payment. Later, I discovered the bill was hundreds of thousands of dollars!

My experiences during that period were surely not conducive to the serenity and healthy physical and emotional development of a teen. I witnessed people restricted in shackles and escorted to the 'rubber room.' This was a closed in area, wallpapered and carpeted in thick black rubber to prevent injury when patients went ballistic.

Passing through the halls, I'd see nurses running after out-of-control kids, with hypodermic needles in their hands ready to inject them with what we called 'vitamin h' shots. Supposedly this would deliver a tranquilizer to allow them to be shackled and or strapped down to a bed or chair and escorted to the rubber room.

Although it was neither a brutality nor abuse issue due to the wild, violent nature of the children involved and the potential harm they could inflict on themselves and others, it was at first surprising to see this scene repeated on a daily basis. Ultimately, it became a commonplace eventuality.

The kids would be monitored and once the self aimed insurrection ended, taken back to their rooms.

Once again observing this sad scenario on a daily basis, I kept receiving the confirmation that there was nothing wrong with me.

Four months later I was discharged. However, when Mr. Qubicz received the news from Dr. Marsh, he was dismayed about my time spent in the mental facility—certainly not a very intellectually or emotionally stimulating environment for a sixteen-year-old dealing with her own issues.

Chapter 5

My Dignity Borne Off on the Wind

"My spirit is broken, my lamp of light
extinguished; my burial is at hand.
I am indeed mocked, and as their
provocation mounts, my eyes grow dim."
—Job17:1-2

What happened to the rainbow? Where is all the hope and excitement quickening the pulse of a young girl just several years shy of adulthood? Where are the exhilarating wishes and plans for tomorrow—for the rest of my life? What will my journey be like? Where am I going from here? Or do I even want to know?

My mind was plagued with a multitude of doubts and unknowns and so many unanswerable questions for which I was often afraid to hear a response. Familiarity was synonymous with neglect, an indelibly scarring rejection and an abuse-saturated culture that torched my self-respect in small doses day by day.

I had nowhere to go—no place to call home. No one was available to listen to me or calm my fears and anxieties. I had neither support nor guidance—a complete disengagement of parental intervention. But worst of all, I felt loved by no one.

A heavy darkness invaded my body, boring a huge empty hole that seemed to be a fate I had to accept, even if unwillingly. Was a bright sunny day just a double-crossing mirage?

After my discharge from South Wood, I was once again inserted in the Juvenile Crisis Resolution Program while the authorities searched for a suitable foster care alternative.

Since my parents held firm in their conviction that I was 'incorrigible,' Mr. Qubicz was once again assigned as my counselor. Firm and unwavering in his belief, Uncle George insisted, "Under no circumstances will I allow Margaret to move back into the house. She is incorrigible and I cannot control her—so she needs to live elsewhere."

Shortly after my arrival at the JCRP, I received a visit from Mr.Qubicz. Ever pleasant and congenial, he said, smiling broadly, "Margaret we've found a foster family for you."

But joy was an outsider, an inadmissible stranger to me. My previous experiences familiarized me only with disappointment and misery. Therefore, I listened to his words with disbelief and the unaffected reaction of a child accustomed to broken promises. Straight-faced, I nodded my approval and went to pack my belongings.

As is customary, Mr. Qubicz accompanied me to my new foster family. From the simplistic, two bedroom home that greeted me upon our arrival, it was apparent money was tight.

We walked along a cracked concrete path where hordes of ants seemed to be parading up and down, undisturbed by our presence. I noticed how orderly they were and how determined to reach their destination. They seemed headed in the same direction in which we were traveling. Not one dared stray the course.

Before the echo of Mr.Qubicz's knock had quieted, the door flew open with a loud squeak. For a brief moment I shuddered, remembering the awful squeals of my bedroom mice with their heads caught in the traps my mother had set.

A middle-aged woman stood in the doorway. With shoulder length blonde hair and rather ample of figure, she bore an amazing resemblance to Kermit's Miss Piggy! Looking into her beady eyes, I tried to smother a giggle.

She motioned with a thick, stubby hand, inviting us into the living room. Once inside I noticed the seasoned furnishings showed every trace of wear and tear including large unsightly stains which no one had ever attempted to remove. The walls, once white, were dull and faded, and the now off-white linoleum floor betrayed a secret of poor housekeeping.

The picture of an African American man in a navy uniform stood on a small table next to a lamp with a faded shade, somewhat frayed at the edges.

Noticing my gaze focus on the picture, Miss Piggy blurted, "That's my husband. He's in the navy." I looked but offered no comment. He did seem attractive and looked like an interesting person. However, in my mind's eye, I could not see the two of them as a couple.

"Margaret," Miss Piggy said clearing her throat; "would you like to see your room?" I nodded, smiling demurely. She escorted me to a small bedroom and pointed to a low metal twin bed that time had oxidized almost black.

"This is where you will sleep," she said, not bothering to look at me. "I think you'll find it comfortable."

Unable to shake my depression and incapable of warming to a woman who seemed so unfamiliar and distant, I said good evening, undressed and slipped between the stiff sheets. I planned to remain in bed for two weeks, until this ordeal would be over and done with.

Disoriented, I also felt embarrassed by my surroundings. Oddly, life at the South Wood Mental Health Facility, once my roommate was discharged, had become a great deal better. Undisturbed by the presence of another, I was at liberty to experience a bit of privacy. Simultaneously, the facility offered more opportunity for companionship and independence despite the barbed wire fencing at the entry. And hailing from a middle class family, I was accustomed to a bit more luxury than Miss Piggy's lifestyle provided.

Feeling isolated and lonely with a weighty chunk of sadness trapped in my chest, I had little energy or ambition to explore my new surroundings.

Miss Piggy had a little son who was barely older than a toddler—definitely not of the age to interact with a teenage girl. Rarely, if ever did I see him even walk by my room, let alone stick his head in to say hello. To him I did not even exist!

After two days of seclusion, Miss Piggy came to my room. "Margaret," she said, denying me even an insincere smile, "you cannot stay in here all the time. You have to get out of bed. You have to eat something. Get dressed—my husband's fleet is in, and I'd like you to come with me to visit him."

Perhaps she believed that once removed from my current surroundings even for an afternoon, I would be enlivened and encouraged to participate more in life instead of choosing to remain comatose in my room.

However, at the time, I felt misplaced in this biracial family. Thankfully, what is no longer a head-turner today was still the exception twenty-five years ago. Furthermore, I was well aware of the $1,100 monthly recompense paid to individuals who committed to taking in foster children.

In the program in which I was enrolled, children assigned to a family were not permitted to attend school. Instead, they were obliged to remain always in the company of the foster parent. Therefore, for the duration of my stay with Miss Piggy, my fate was to be her sidekick, an idea I vehemently rejected. In my mind, I was nothing more than her part-time job!

After my several weeks of barely existing, Mr. Qubicz returned for a visit. Apparently distressed with my deepening depression and failure to acclimate myself in my surroundings, he found another temporary foster home he thought might be more suitable until permanent accommodations would be available.

"I have another place for you," Mr. Qubicz said, patting my shoulder, "and I think you might find it better suited. There are five other foster girls your age living there, so you'll have a bit of company." Eager to leave Miss Piggy, I gathered my possessions, said my goodbyes and left for a new adventure.

More questions—more uncertainties: How long will this journey continue? And was there really a destination? Confused I asked myself—"but where exactly am I going?"

The unknowns remained as such, untouched and unresolved. One thing was certain—I walked alone, making eye contact with no one and nothing but the ground upon which I tread. Conversations were mostly with myself—solitary monologues. Questions seemed to stumble on deafened ears, abandoned and left unanswered. I just didn't get it. What was this all about?

It was Mr. Qubicz's opinion that I would be able to shake my depression if placed in a situation where I would have the company and solidarity of girls my own age in my same predicament.

What remained an unknown to Mr. Qubicz, I learned as soon as I entered my new foster home—the five girls with whom I would share my days were rough, brutally bold, ethically challenged and tumultuously violent individuals whose only agreeable social interaction was with each other.

Thankfully, not all foster children fit this profile. However, in this house I was definitely out of my league. Admitted and released numerous times from Juvenile Hall, the girls were tough, resentful, angry and aggressively defensive.

We shared a rather commonplace, characterless room decorated with three sets of dark wood bunk beds that bore scars of mistreatment—perhaps from angry rampages accompanied by a few swift 'temper tantrum' kicks to the frames.

It was obvious the girls were territorial, and I was the last to march in. Our foster mother had announced my arrival, explaining a bit of my background, which apparently led them to label me a 'trouble maker.' Consequently, I started off disliked and blacklisted.

And as the unfavorable newcomer, I was the butt of their nasty comments and offensive name-calling. Emotionally and psychologically bullied, I felt intimidated and disheartened from the first moment.

Our foster mother was by her own designation a 'practicing witch.' A fifty-ish physician's wife of comfortable means with a prominent middle-years' roundness, she had a huge, protruding bulbous nose. Her long auburn hair was not particularly attractive on her time-scarred face. In fact, her overall demeanor fell into the perfect stereotype of a storybook witch.

After Mr. Qubicz helped me take my luggage to the room, we said our goodbyes. In contrast to mine, his face was at ease and serene. "Margaret," he said, reassuringly, "I think you will be happy here. I'll be back next week to check up on you."

I turned and headed back to my room. "I want to show you around," the witch said, interrupting my own train of thoughts. "When you're settled in come back to the family room."

"OK," I responded with little enthusiasm. I had already noticed the single story contemporary white-shingled house was built high on a hill surrounded by over fifty acres of land. It was somewhat grandiose and well decorated. When Mr. Qubicz and I entered through the large double entry doors, my eyes focused on a colossal brick and stone circular fireplace centered in the middle of the family room. I had to admit the witch lived in a perfect setting.

Several minutes later I joined the girls and the witch around the fireplace. Her reason for the meeting was an 'initiation and orientation'—to learn the rules and regulations of the house.

Madame Witch was clear and direct in her presentation. "House rule number one," she emphasized, pointing a gnarled finger in the direction of a long, shadowy corridor, "you are not permitted to walk down this hallway." Following her finger with my eyes, I saw that the hall in question had painted white walls and red-gray shag carpeting.

One of the girls leaned over, whispering, "The hallway is haunted with ghosts and evil spirits. If you dare disobey the witch's orders you will suffer a violent, untimely death."

I kept my eyes on the witch, thinking, *This woman is a 'wacko' and she comes with five nasty girls!*

Just as I had anticipated, not long thereafter, the girls grabbed hold of me one day and shoved me down the outlawed, foreboding hallway. Petrified, I lost my footing and fell to my knees, emitting bloodcurdling screams. Although the witch's threat of an 'untimely death' did not materialize, I felt an icy chill as a cold blast of air filled the seemingly 'haunted' hallway. Standing at attention with their arms interlocked, the girls blocked any escape I could have possibly attempted.

When the witch came running the girls pulled away, clearing the entry. Reassuring her I had not come of my own accord, despite their protestations, she gave their version credence over my victim testimony of claiming to have been pushed against my will.

Irritated and angered, she yanked me by the arm. "Go to your room," she shouted, "you're on restriction for the rest of the day."

That evening a frightening nightmare about the witch's haunted hallway invaded my sleep. Ghosts sprang from the darkness encircling me within their tightly interlocked hands. I tried to duck and run between their legs, but my feet seemed cemented to the floor. Soaked in the icy sweat of fear, I awakened to a rapidly thumping heart.

The following day around five o'clock, I walked into the family room to join the witch and the other girls all seated around the fireplace for what she called cocktail hour. She seemed somewhat tipsy and was nurturing a glass of scotch. I soon discovered she was more than an occasional drinker, and when she told us her story I learned the motive.

"On Christmas Eve," she began, pausing at intervals to sip her cocktail, "while returning from the hospital, my husband called me from his cell phone to announce his imminent arrival. While we chatted his auto was hit by a speeding, out of control vehicle."

I sat on the edge of my chair waiting to hear the rest of the witch's story.

She told us that she heard the initial impact of the crash, followed by spine-tingling sounds of crushed metal and shattered glass. Shouting his name into the phone she bore witness to deep breathing and ear-piercing moans that spoke of unimaginable agony.

In the background people were yelling for ambulances. His moans and groans turned into whimpers, becoming gradually soundless like the slowly fading echoes of coastal pelicans fleeing the sea at dusk. Calling his name repeatedly, she received one last sigh before he died. Drinking heavily, she stared into space upon finishing her recountal. Taking on a far away look she proceeded to tell us about her witchcraft and ability to cast spells on people, claiming she was a white magic witch. If her intention was to scare me, I'd have to say her endeavors were successful.

Realizing I was living in a witch's house petrified me. Not daring to cross her in any way imaginable, I walked around as if my feet were trailblazing along a path of slippery ice.

My anxiety level had increased and I was feeling uneasy. One morning I approached the witch, asking, "Can I send a message to Mr. Qubicz?" speaking calmly to conceal my nervousness. "No, that will not be possible," she retorted, never bothering to give an explanation. I knew he had been on vacation, but I also knew that as his assistant, Janet would be available in his absence.

"Come here, now," she shouted without addressing anyone in particular, "it's time to start picking the avocados. They are ripe and ready." This was our 'chore' under the hot sun, eight hours a day. We were her full-time labor force—only she was collecting the money!

The witch had acres of distant avocado groves, about a mile from the house. Once she got us all together, we went over to the groves. "Climb up," she ordered pointing to some massive trees.

Grabbing hold of a branch I tried to lift myself off the ground. Gazing down at my feet, I spotted a long, green and black scaly snake flexing to the right and left as it slithered past my right foot. In the midday sunlight its rippled skin appeared almost iridescent. It moved cautiously, like a graceful cougar ready to spring on his prey.

Frozen in terror, I held my breath until I noticed an extended pitch-fork like tongue sprout from what I perceived to be the snake's mouth. Just as it was about to slam into my foot, I turned and darted back towards the house.

Although at the time I didn't know if the snake was venomous, I was eventually informed the area was heavily populated with reptiles. One thing was certain—I was living with a witch in a house with a haunted hallway and a back yard crawling with snakes! Furthermore, she was using foster care to gain slave labor.

That evening I was grounded for evading my job as avocado picker. "You will stay in your room until it's time to go back to the groves tomorrow," the witch said.

"But there are snakes out there," I blurted. "I'm afraid of those snakes. They bite and they are poisonous!"

Much as I protested, my desperate pleas fell on deafened ears and a cold heart. The following day we were sent back to the groves to pick avocados. Again, I witnessed the presence of snakes and once again I took off. This time I ran as far away from the house as possible.

Without a destination in mind and uncertain of my unfamiliar surroundings, I was interested only in putting as much distance as possible between me and the snake-infested groves. Consequently, driven by emotion and not reason, I got hopelessly lost until the witch found me.

I was in 'serious' trouble and given a sentence to match my crime. Locked in the laundry room with her two menacing Doberman guard dogs, I sat on a narrow plastic chair, not daring to blink an eye. My 'cellmates' were muscular, dark brown animals—intimidating creatures with alert, 'not willing to miss anything,' almond-shaped eyes that controlled every breath I took.

The dogs were well trained to obey the witch's commands. Before shutting the door, she shouted, "Attack if she moves!" I was trembling and scared to tremble, knowing one tiny movement would turn me into snack food for the potentially ferocious Dobermans.

When I lifted my hand to scratch an itch on my ear, I heard a chorus of thundering growls accompanied by the exhibition of two full sets of pearly white canine teeth—long, thin snatching and perforating fangs, gnawing incisors and flesh-shearing, bone-shattering molars.

One glance told me they were already salivating for my young, tender limbs. Much as the witch's Dobermans were quite stately and beautiful to look at, I was starring in a rather distressful scenario!

The witch had told me not to move at all—not even to relieve the call of nature. "Don't move if you don't want to be eaten alive. And if you have to relieve yourself—do it in your pants," she shouted before taking leave and slamming the door shut.

Terrified of my Doberman 'companions,' I sat completely still, struggling to keep my inhalations and exhalations as shallow as possible to keep from fainting, but more importantly to assure myself the dogs would remain disengaged!

I felt an aching tightness in my neck and back and a tingling in my legs. Tiny beads of sweat were sailing across my brow, dripping down the sides of my cheeks. I kept my hands as still as possible, interlocked and crossed in my lap.

I lowered my gaze to the floor, not wanting to provoke the dogs in any way imaginable. A prevailing graveyard silence was interrupted by an occasional paw scratching to death an invading flea.

It was a miracle I did not slip into cardiac arrest. First it was the awful snakes and now the vicious Dobermans.

Seated motionless for five hours, like a wax sculpture attached to a hard-surfaced chair, I had plenty of time to ponder my new fate: "I think I'm in a lot of trouble," I said to myself. "Where have I ended up, now! Will it ever end?"

Once reprieved of my sentence, I was freed from the doghouse. "I must phone Mr. Qubicz," I told the witch when she came to liberate me. "I need to talk to him." Once again requests were denied. Smiling and patting her Dobermans on their heads, she broke in, "The next time you run away, I will make certain the dogs will attack and no one will ever find your remains. Is that clear?"

I didn't dignify her question with an agreement, a disagreement or a rebellious comment. Instead, shrugging my shoulders, I put a distance between us.

It didn't take a brilliant mind to discover the witch was a wicked, reprehensible, and heartless woman. Thankfully,

Mr. Qubicz returned from his vacation and came to visit as promised. Relieved to see him, I suggested we go for a walk instead of chatting in the evil house.

Once out under the noonday sky, I told him about my week with the witch, omitting not even the most trivial examples of her detestable behavior. "She wouldn't even allow me to phone you or Janet," I said. "This woman is mean and evil, and I'm scared to live here. I want to leave."

When Mr. Qubicz reported my comments to the witch, she denied every accusation and or allegation I had made of abuse and ill-conduct on her part.

"Oh, Bill," she blurted, when confronted, "Margaret is like all the foster kids—they have wild imaginations and tell lies."

"Well," Mr. Qubicz said, jumping to my defense, "I have never known Margaret to make up stories before."

Surprised by the idea of someone actually coming to my defense, I experienced a new feeling of support. Customarily, I felt only emptiness, darkness and a repeatedly pointed finger condemning me for being a bad girl. Words either spoke of my naughty deeds or informed me of my punishment. So, hearing Mr. Qubicz say I was not a liar startled me.

Refusing his defense, the witch summoned the other five girls to bring testimony against me. Of course, they obliged, one by one swearing about the legitimacy of my evil nature and deeds—confirming all her accusations.

Unfortunately, Mr. Qubicz was swayed by the 'witnesses' and their false testimony, never pausing a moment to consider the 'perjury factor.'

"Margaret," he said afterwards, "I'm very disappointed in you. I didn't expect this behavior and don't know what to do with you. Honestly, I don't have another foster home to send you to. I'm doing my best to find you a permanent place. But, in the meantime you'll just have to stick it out."

I felt so lost and alone and totally worthless—even Mr. Qubicz didn't have any faith in me. There was no trust. How could he believe I had lied? The already cool temperature of the long empty tunnel within, took another nosedive. Would anyone ever really care for me? I felt so hollow inside: Dead.

In keeping with the original plan, I spent another week in the witch's custody. The environment was tense, and one day after ingesting several tall glasses of scotch, she made a nasty, derogatory comment that just rubbed me the wrong way.

"You're a psychotic witch," I screamed, enraged. "You're pure evil. I have never met another woman as wicked and devious as you. You're nothing but a miserable wretch—that's why your husband died on you—that is if you didn't kill him yourself!"

Ruthless, I continued my verbal assault without any hint of a ceasefire. Visibly agitated, she turned and left the room. Later, I heard she gave the five girls permission to physically attack and maim me at will. However, a strange alliance had sprung forth. Perhaps the girls realized how malicious and dangerous she was, when intoxicated or sober or hungover.

"Don't talk to her," one of the girls said, "and she'll leave you alone. We don't want any trouble. This is one of the best homes in which I have lived and I don't want anything to happen to spoil my stay here."

Her surprising reaction didn't speak very highly of her foster care experiences up until now. If life with the witch was the best, I thought, shuddering, what were the others like?

Upset and rattled by my defiant outburst, the witch decided it was time for me to pack up and move on. Until now she had been able to control and manipulate the other girls and so now feared my aggressive rampage might trigger a rebellious uprising. And there was absolutely no way she could ever handle five mutinous teenage girls.

Finally. Mr. Qubicz phoned, giving me the good news I could pack my belongings. The following day he came to pick me up. During our drive to my new foster home he confessed, "Margaret I believe you had a terrible time there. I know you were telling the truth. They set you up."

Apparently, unbeknown to the witch, one of the other girls had spoken in confidence to her counselor, reporting the malicious goings-on in witch-land.

With my credibility no longer challenged, I hoped at least justice would be served. There was no happiness in my life, but with every new foster family I visited, perhaps things would get at least better—maybe even less agonizing.

Chapter 6

Flight of the Ebony Dove

"Come take your wife and your two daughters here, lest you perish in the punishment of the City. Flee for your life; do not look behind you or stop anywhere in the valley; flee to the hills, lest you perish."
—Genesis 19:15-17

It was time to spread my wings and take off again on the next lap of my foster care journey. Mr. Qubicz accompanied me to a new foster home where I was scheduled to remain for a brief period of time until a permanent family was found. Though unwilling to hope, I was excited by the new possibility of being sent to a better home.

Marilyn, a warm agreeable soul with fiery red hair and blue penetrating eyes received me with a genuine smile. She made it known she was happy to accept me for the duration of the time, so I would not have to play musical chairs every few weeks.

When she showed me to my room, I was pleasantly surprised. Although the family was far from wealthy, she had done an excellent job making the area welcoming with pastel floral bedding and window treatments. It was a serene room, inviting and attractive, and I would eventually share it with another foster girl.

In contrast to Miss Piggy and the witch, Marilyn was a kindhearted, loquacious woman with a strong Christian faith. Tall and statuesque, her presence was noted.

Marilyn began to fascinate me. Different from the other foster ladies, she seemed so book-dependent and walked around carrying a large leather bound book that seemed to be worn from over-reading. An avid reader myself, I wondered what enthralling things were nestled within those pages to warrant her reading all the time.

When she awakened she took the book in hand. At lunch time she paged through it again. In the evening she read some more, and before retiring she would sit with her nose buried in the pages.

"Marilyn," I asked one day, unable to curtail my curiosity, "what are you reading all the time?"

"The Bible," she responded, raising her eyes to catch my glance. "I'm reading the Bible—the words of God."

Oddly enough, I had overheard several discussions between her and her husband in which he had adamantly chastised her for believing in the Divine Presence. He was neither secretive nor inhibited about pronouncing hatred for the Bible and God.

A Border Patrol Guard stationed in San Diego, he would never accompany her to church on Sundays. Instead, he alienated himself from God with the same furor and passion in which she embraced Him.

After these angry spats she would sit, flushed and breathing heavily, open her Bible and read aloud in soft whispers, sometimes shutting her eyes between passages. Moments later her knotted brow would untangle, her tightened jaw, relax and an enviable wave of calm would loosen her shoulders and steady her hands. During those moments she seemed so happy and at peace.

Puzzled, I wondered what she could be reading that would have such a transforming effect on her. She seemed like another woman.

"Margaret," she said one afternoon after lunch, "I'd like to take you to church with me on Sunday. I want to enroll you in the Youth Ministry. There is a nice couple, Gary and Tammy, I'd like you to meet. They are young and very active in the church. I think you will enjoy their company."

I was excited not only by the possibility of going somewhere different from Juvenile Hall, mental hospitals, rehab programs, and mean foster homes, but by the idea that someone was taking me to a nice place for a change. Maybe Marilyn liked me! Was she able to see some good in me? No one else did until now. I was punished and beaten and told I was mentally ill and unwanted. "Incorrigible"— that's what Uncle George said over and over again.

I was still not permitted to attend school, and in keeping with the rules I was not allowed to be out of her sight; therefore, I was obliged to accompany Marilyn to all her Bible Study groups and on her missionary expeditions.

A Witness for Jesus, she would travel from house to house bringing Jesus to others by speaking of Christ the Redeemer and encouraging them to pray with her. Quoting from her Bible, she'd say:

"For the wages of sin is death, but the gift of God
is life everlasting in Christ Jesus our Lord."
—Romans 6:23

Marilyn's main focus was to convert to Christianity unbelievers or believers from other faiths. Most of the homes we visited were inhabited by Middle-Easterners and she would introduce them to the crucified Christ and the salvation of humanity through suffering and death.

At sixteen years of age, totally ignorant of all religious doctrines and teachings, I thought Marilyn was beyond wacky. I had never heard anyone speak in this manner before and did not understand one word of what she was referring to in her dialogues.

However, despite my spiritual ignorance, I was surprised by the genial and indulgent reception she received from whomever she visited. It was amazing to observe how complete strangers could be so open and receptive to her presence.

At home she was a caring parent figure, preparing evening meals for her family, gaining gratification from the illumination of their satisfied smiles. A 'domestic skills-challenged' teen, Marilyn took the time to explain and demonstrate the aspects of meal planning and preparation as well as other useful and essential household things.

She taught me how to wash, cut and cook vegetables, and make spicy mayonnaise mustard dressing with fresh dill. Her manner was interesting and she was quite adept at her 'trade.'

Throughout the years I have 'borrowed' many of her wonderful recipes, in particular her delicious macaroni salad, which later in my adult life were and are always well received among my family and friends. The recipes she taught may have seemed basic, but people certainly enjoyed them.

Feeling sorry for my practically nonexistent domestic skills, she also taught me how to do some very basic stitching and to re-attach buttons. Without funds for a store-bought wardrobe, she had to learn how to make her own clothing.

Life at Marilyn's was quite a refreshing change from the life I led for sixteen years. However, the serene environment was disturbed by the presence of her husband, a man who would not tolerate even the name of God in his home. It was such an absurd inconsistency—a deeply committed Christian woman who lived and breathed by the Bible, and a contrary spouse who would not support any manifestations or mention of God.

Feeling her faith deeply, Marilyn would sometimes let her soul fly free, speaking about and giving praise to her Divine Savior. Enraged, her husband would become flushed. His myopic eyes fortressed behind dark-rimmed glasses would narrow to slits, furrowing his brow. "I'll have none of that God stuff," he'd shout, slamming his fist on the table. I work all day and till late in the evenings; I'm tired and I'm hungry and I want to eat my dinner without any of this crazy nonsense!"

Marilyn would just bow her head, command her anguish to silence and finish her meal. I didn't understand what all the fuss was about, though I wondered about this unknown God and why mentioning Him would cause such a ruckus. Perhaps they were both whacky! Why didn't they fight about more normal things, I'd question silently.

Sometimes Marilyn's husband worked the graveyard shift. During those periods his daytime sleeping gave her the freedom to go about as a missionary witnessing Jesus. Of course, she prayed for her husband often and I believe she would implore Jesus to help him receive the light. It was all bizarre to me.

Ignorant of her Jesus, I wondered why she squandered so much time speaking about *Someone* we could neither see nor talk to. Though I believed Marilyn was a total nut job, I had to admit I liked her. Poles apart from anyone I knew, this kind lady treated me with respect—like a human being.

Unable to attend school, my social life was limited to Marilyn and her family. However, we had built a relationship of trust. Accompanying her to church on Sundays, I was encouraged to mingle with the other teenagers in the congregation. Joining the youth ministry brought me to Gary and his wife, Tammy.

Gary was a twenty-two-year-old, handsome, tall, slim youth minister with dark hair and vibrant green eyes—perfect for the protagonist of a passionate love story. Tammy, his wife, an equally beautiful young woman who possessed the physical attributes of a *haute couture* runway model, was the mother of his two-year-old son.

Recognizing I was a foster child, he dedicated a great deal more of his time to me, seeding jealousy in the other youth group girls. Consequently, they distanced themselves, refusing to befriend me. However, besieged by the devastating events of my first sixteen years, Gary found my situation incredibly overwhelming and felt it was his mission to intervene.

The repeated neglect, the shocking abuse, the disturbing rejection and the total absence of any spiritual knowledge were beyond appalling. "How could this happen?" he said to Tammy. "I can't believe the dreadful life this young girl has lived. She doesn't attend school and she has no faith!"

Upset, he approached me one Sunday. "Margaret," he said, protectively cradling my hand, as a father would a child's, "I think that if you were baptized and accepted Jesus as your Savior, your life would change."

"We cannot force her to be baptized," Marilyn interjected, upon hearing his words. "She has to want to embrace the faith and get baptized of her own wishes or it will not do her any good."

I had no idea what they were talking about, but felt once again that they were all somewhat crazy, even if kind and likeable. It was agreed that I would continue to frequent the church, attend the dinners and socialize with the other teens.

I assume Gary had given the other members a summary of my profile, and much to my surprise and delight they took me under their wings.

Could I trust all the smiles and endearing words? Were there really good people in this world? Did others really care about me? Was I worthy of all the attention?

With love and kindness a rarity, I questioned the sudden change in my life. Could I accept it? Or would rejection come careening down into my face as it always did?

Since my stay with Marilyn was part of the temporary program, a permanent foster care arrangement had to be found—however, until that occurred I would remain in her custody.

Upon returning home from church one Sunday, Marilyn received news of a death in the family. Petitioning the courts, she asked for permission to bring me out of state for a couple of weeks. Her request was denied.

"I'm sorry you cannot come with us," she said through pursed lips, "but I promise you that as soon as we're back, I'll bring you home with us." It sounded somewhat reassuring to me. *Two weeks will pass quickly*, I thought to myself.

The following day, Marilyn accompanied me to Juvenile Hall. When the car pulled to a halt in front of the austere building, I shuddered. Flashbacks invaded my mind—upsetting memories of what I had hoped would remain buried in another time. She slid out from behind the wheel and walked over to the passenger side, extending her hand to open the door just as I lifted the handle to get out.

I looked directly at her as a huge white cloud danced towards the horizon, uncovering a radiant sun; a sun whose illumination betrayed the sadness in her heart. In the light of day, I noticed her eyes brimming over with tears. Even the swiftness of her hand could not wipe away the glistening flow.

Leaning forward, she gave me a hug. "I'll be back for you soon," she whispered.

Once inside I was stripped, searched and showered down with a pungent smelling disinfectant to kill any lice I may have contracted. A guard handed me a set of scrubs to put on.

I was now in the company of convicted, hardened criminals and illegal aliens guilty of serious gang activities. I looked and was treated as one of these dangerous individuals, whose mindset involved neither scruples nor remorse or the slightest concept of right or wrong.

Consequently, every day began with a threat and survival was a constant battle. Even locked and bolted behind bars, my safety was at risk. I had to forfeit my meals to the criminal bullies in exchange for being saved from terrible beatings.

A lost soul, confused and alone, I realized this devastating, humiliating life was not the life I wanted. Therefore, to maintain my freedom, I promised myself I would be super-cautious never to break the law.

After five days my grandmother Donna found out I was back in Juvenile Hall. She petitioned for custody until Marilyn's return. Much to my surprise her request was granted and she presented herself to pick me up as soon as she received the OK. I was rescued!

When I saw Grandma Donna coming through the door, I ran hurling myself at her. Steadying herself to avoid a fall, she locked her arms around me. "I'm so happy to see you, Grandma, I miss you so much!" I shouted.

She hugged me without letting me catch my breath. "You can stay with me until Marilyn gets back."

I was delirious. My dear grandmother was beside herself, "What am I going to do with you?" she said, sighing. "How can I get you back on track?"

Exasperated by the turbulent unraveling of my life, she doted on me giving me an abundance of love and attention. We spent a wonderful week together catching up and enjoying each others company, and when it was time to return to my foster home, she helped me gather my things. Maintaining her end of the agreement, Grandma Donna drove me back to the Juvenile Crisis Resolution Program, even if reluctantly, with a heavy heart and tear-filled eyes.

We pulled up to the entrance, parked the car and walked inside. I was not surprised to see Mr. Qubicz, waiting to accompany me to Marilyn's.

I gazed at my grandmother and before I could speak she locked her arms around me, "It'll be OK, Margaret," she whispered. "Just do as you are told. You may not understand now, but this is only a small stage in your life. And Marilyn seems like a nice lady. I'm sure she will take good care of you."

'Just a small stage in my life'—I repeated over and over. My grandmother's words became a type of mantra for difficult moments in life and always reminded and remind me of the truth.

"*Let nothing disturb you. Let nothing afrighten you. All things are passing. God only is changeless.*"

St. Theresa of Avila's Book Mark Prayer

I returned to Marilyn's for another two weeks while Grandmother Donna continued to petition the courts for visitation rights. She had tried for over a year, but since I was part of the state system and had been completely removed from my family, her requests were repeatedly denied.

Shortly thereafter I was informed that a permanent foster family had been found. This meant life would take on a more normal spin, and I would be allowed to return to school and the social activities teenagers enjoy. The identity of this family escapes me. In time, as part of my healing process, I have deleted from my memory some of the painful and toxic aspects of my turbulent years. Rejecting negative thoughts, I try to focus on what I learned from my horrendous experiences instead of concentrating on the actual agonizing torture.

I do recall that this set of foster parents was a French Creole couple from New Orleans. The gentleman by profession was a postman in Chula Vista and the woman was running full speed in a midlife crisis complete with hormonal dives and resulting characteristic behavioral repercussions, which at the time I did not understand. Teenage girls usually don't focus on menopause since puberty is a difficult enough process to deal with.

Although in no way abusive, she lived on an emotional roller coaster, often out of control. However, the couple had a new brown-wood, shingle-track home, left in its natural state. Unlike the previous homes, each room was professionally decorated with color coordinated enhancements. Some rooms had shiny, hard wood floors, others had soft to the touch wall-to-wall carpeting, and the bathrooms were tiled in various hues to match the fixtures.

The furnishings were up-scale and an aura of immaculate cleanliness prevailed—without the aroma of harsh smelling disinfectants and detergents.

The couple's two daughters were grown and on their own. They would visit from time to time, but found it exasperating to deal with a mother in eternal menopausal crisis.

At first I was concerned it was another wacky house. Then I started to wonder if maybe I was not 'all there.' Could it be possible that everyone was nuts! Everyone I had visited was weird—or was it me?

I started to take to heart the awful things said on my behalf. Perhaps they were all true. Maybe I was incorrigible.

Then my thoughts would be interrupted. The Creole woman would be screaming and crying, slamming doors while her husband, frayed to the bones, would isolate himself in another part of the house, clueless that his distancing behavior only intensified her raging outbursts and feelings of abandonment.

I felt sorry for him. He worked all day and wanted some peace, loving company and attention when he returned in the evenings.

In my regard they were agreeable and tried to do the best despite the extenuating upheavals. I was back in school in a continuation program structured for dropouts and made new friends. Life seemed to have normalized somewhat.

Meanwhile, Marilyn, who lived just a short distance from the Creole couple, had petitioned the family for the authorization to pick me up on Sundays to attend church.

Permission granted, I was allowed to go with Marilyn until they discovered Gary and Tammy had petitioned for my custody as permanent foster parents.

Upset by this unexpected turn of events, the Creole woman expressed her disapproval. "Margaret is living with us," she said, "and faring quite well." Infuriated with Marilyn, she felt betrayed. Rebutting, she negated her approval, denying all requests for church visits.

Shortly thereafter she came into my room. "Margaret," she said, "get dressed, I'm taking you to the dermatologist for checkup." Puzzled, I complied. When we arrived I was invited into the doctor's study and asked to strip naked. The dermatologist, obviously at the request of my foster mother, administered a gynecological examination. I was poked and probed sore. Feeling violated and humiliated in front of the Creole woman, I questioned why the dermatologist would treat me in this fashion.

It didn't take much brain energy to solve the riddle. Apparently the two women, the MD and my foster mother were in cahoots, and I was being screened for sexually transmitted diseases.

I phoned Mr. Qubicz, spilling out the horrid details of the mortifying experience I had just lived through. He was beside himself, phoned the Creole couple and admonished them for their unacceptable behavior. "This is not permitted," Mr. Qubicz cautioned. "Please do not ever repeat this again."

That evening my foster father knocked on my bedroom door. "Margaret," he whispered, edging his way into the room after I asked him to come in, "I'm sorry about the incident at the dermatologist. I had no idea and would have never given my permission."

Several days later Mr. Qubicz phoned. "Margaret," he said, "Gary and Tammy have been approved as permanent foster parents. Would you like to go and live with them?"

"Yes," I responded, immediately blabbing my approval. I was sixteen years old and, thankfully, did not have to spend much more time playing foster care, Juvenile Hall and JCRP musical chairs.

After five months with the Creoles and much bickering for reasons unknown to me, I was released from their custody and transferred to Gary and Tammy. They lived in a two bedroom, two bathroom home with little financial resources.

The couple had marital problems due to an un-planned pregnancy that forced them to marry at an early age. At just twenty-one and twenty-two years of age, they had two children to support on a youth minister's salary.

In school I was doing pretty well scholastically, but socially I was chastised and mercilessly teased for not being permitted to attend dances or date. Feeling like an outcast, I had little choice but to explain I was living in foster care.

My relationship with Gary and Tammy was pretty solid despite it all. They seemed a bit more understanding—at least at times. Furthermore, this foster home seemed the best of the lot—perhaps because of their young ages.

I still missed my grandmother terribly, and when I learned that my mother and Uncle George were in the process of divorcing, I longed to return home. Through it all, I was unaware my mother had been petitioning for visitation, until it was granted.

Not long after I was allowed to return home for visits. This new freedom presented the opportunity to begin rebuilding our shattered mother-daughter relationship.

However, filled with disappointment and heartache, I was afraid to even hope. At seventeen I was free to make my own decision regarding with whom I would choose to live. Fearing the worst, Gary and Tammy pleaded with me to stay. "Margaret," Gary said looking everywhere but at me, "if you leave us, we will loose the $1,100 a month. And if you agree to stay another six months with us we will allow you to date and enjoy the activities other girls your age do."

My pulse quickened. My stomach churned. I now had the confirmation for what I had begun to suspect—Gary and Tammy in need of financial aid agreed to care for me solely for mercenary reasons. They needed me to keep their house and their position as youth ministers in the church! Recognizing they were trying to bribe me, I was furious and resentful. It was all about dollars and cents that was the mission of my foster care!

By now I had been in ten different foster homes— living with mostly unbalanced individuals who cared exclusively about the financial aspect of foster care. Given neither nurturing nor attention, I never received even one pair of new shoes during these years.

Furthermore, I had been inserted in less than stable environments with people not suitable to undertake the care and guardianship of a young vulnerable minor. They were not willing to even talk to me about my issues or try to offer some support and assistance. It was about the continuation of abuse—from physical at home with Uncle George to emotional with most of my foster care parents.

Yet, the purpose of my foster care experience was to remove me from an environment in which I was not developing properly and place me in a situation in which I could grow and thrive into a healthy, well-adjusted adult and be able to live a dignified life.

Disheartened, I packed my bags and returned home to my mother and Cindy, feeling used and unloved—quivering from the icy cold of a bitter emptiness.

My spirit had been broken—my dignity borne off on the wind!

But—where will I go from here?

> *"Then he sent a dove to see if the waters had abated…But the dove found no place to alight, so she returned to him in the ark… Then he waited another seven days, and sent forth the dove; but she did not return to him any more."*
> —Genesis 8:6-8,12

Exodus

Chapter 7

The Prodigal Daughter Sees God's Glory

"Do let me see your glory! He answered, '
I will make all my beauty pass before you,
and in your presence I will pronounce my name,
'Lord'; I who show favors to whom I will,
I who grant mercy to whom I will."
—Exodus 33:18-19

Bags packed, I was ready for my return to the fold. Uncle George was no longer living with my mother— a thought I found quite reassuring. It was like a cooling breeze invading on a hot humid night. However, the hollowness inside still held me captive in a sinister dungeon. I was living in the 'black hole of Calcutta.'

Misplaced, even from myself, I had no identity. Disconnected from my family I had no answer for the question, "Who am I?" Yet, catching my reflection in the mirror from time to time, I recognized my physical demeanor was a statement not only of the turmoil within, but of the worthlessness with which I defined myself. Still in my teens, I had the bearing of a woman whose life was all knotted in a memory, instead of ready to be inscribed in a book.

The next question was—how do I defeat the enemy within? How do I stop the demons from gnawing at my insides? How do I rid myself of the unwanted feelings of seclusion and abandonment, emptiness and hopelessness, sadness and despair? Where do I go after this agonizing 'dark night of the soul?'

There had to be more. There had to be something else—but what? My life until now was filled with misery, rejection, cruelty and a frustrating sense of groping and hoping for nothing. Why? Because I just didn't have the energy to bear another disillusionment and disappointment. Yet, observing the smiling young faces around me, I wondered if I, too, would one day have a perfect life instead of this meaningless succession of days, months and years which I lived with hate and a fearful mistrust of humanity.

It was one foster home after another—one more possibility to get kicked down and pulled in half. It was one more opportunity to confront the truth; I was unwanted—unloved.

No longer able to see the radiance of the sunrise, I was deafened to the sounds of life. The birds didn't sing, children lost their innocent giggles, and the brilliance of day ran blindly into the dimness of night without ever showing its first morning glow.

I inhaled and exhaled, my heart beat, I walked and I talked, I ate and I drank—but I had no personality, no direction, no spirit and no life. Margaret the bubbly, outgoing 'cheerleader' had disappeared. Margaret the open, extroverted girl who loved to chatter almost round the clock was silenced. I was invisible; just a nobody among many some-bodies.

Convincing myself that being myself equated with accusations of delinquency, guilt and severe punishment, I altered my behavior, withdrawing a little bit more whenever I was moved to a new foster house. In the sometimes strange surroundings of these often abusive people, I battled for survival.

After awhile, I drifted with the currents, taking my cues from the different host families that agreed to take me in.

Though not clinically diagnosed with multiple-personality syndrome, I did assume various personalities for convenience, according to the environment in which I found myself. It was in a sense the confirmation that I was a fragmented individual, deserted, dispersed and shorn of any worth. Overwhelmed, I realized I was in way over my head. Would I be able to overcome even this insurmountable obstacle? I was determined not be defeated—but I had to go beyond just intention and resolve.

Crossing the threshold, I began a new life at home as the prodigal daughter, whose behavior had been deemed beyond the acceptable realm. When the door opened to welcome me, I had little if any expectations and absolutely no direction. Fully aware I had been an absent daughter for years, I felt a sudden swell of envy, realizing Cindy and my mother had formed a loving parent-child bond while I journeyed through a long, dark tunnel filled with obstacles—breeding more misgivings about the world around me.

However, observing them together, I soon discovered a source of happiness swiveling through the hatred. Although it was a different feeling, I had to admit it created a sense of pleasure I found rather appealing.

I had felt this surge once before, when I discovered my mother had petitioned the courts for visitation rights. It seemed as if a wave of soothing warm water had seeped into my body, drowning the chunks of ice as it meandered through my limbs before settling around my heart.

Unable to put words to the feeling, I shrugged it off doubting it would return, yet hopeful it might. And it did. Slowly as the days passed I seemed to see my surroundings in a new light. Thoughts of Marilyn and her Bible returned at unusual intervals, and I kept hearing her voice reciting specific passages.

Until now, God and I were strangers. His name may have been in my mind as a result of the bickering between Marilyn and her non-believing husband, but His presence was not a part of my being.

However, as my character changed from rebellious and disorderly to more accommodating and conventional, I questioned if it was the influence of the abusive foster families or perhaps another force I had not yet reckoned with.

A distinctively vague, indefinable energy guided me down a wider, brighter path. Gazing up at the sky, I noticed massive formations of dark clouds disappearing behind the horizon. I stood in the radiance of unobstructed sunlight feeling as if a huge weight had been lifted from my shoulders.

I did not frequent religious friends or organizations and was certainly not a student of any structured spiritual education. Except for Marilyn's readings and the Sundays spent in church where I took the opportunity to daydream and try to sort out my oppressive existence, I had no spiritual connections.

Then as I began to develop and change, I realized the sudden presence of an indefinable force. Perhaps it was with me all along, but I was just too consumed with wrath and desperation to recognize its existence.

Then the curtain of darkness obscuring my inner vision was lifted. With a subtle bolt of lightening I was awakened to the majesty of God. Able to acknowledge He had taken over the misguided life of a previous spiritual fugitive, my unconscious tussle with accepting Divine influence came to a victorious end.

Unable to pinpoint the exact moment of my life-altering epiphany or rationalize the step by step process, I was too enamored with my newfound 'gift' to squander time and thoughts trying to figure it out.

What mattered was that God had revealed Himself to me in my most dire moment, rescuing me from the abyss into which I had fallen. In time, I had been re-created by the demeaning opinions of others and defined by the consequences of years of neglect, mistreatment and rejection. Furthermore, my freedom to be a lighthearted, happy child was tightly muzzled behind a 'convenient' diagnosis of mental illness.

My new special effervescence gave me the force to embrace the truth—I had a loyal Ally who would love me unconditionally, even if I was incorrigible or chattered incessantly.

Initially I had faith neither in religion nor the church. I believed in the existence of a Powerful Presence, the knowledge of which I attributed exclusively to the intervention of the Holy Spirit, since I had no religious education. Therefore, I did not have any inclination to join a formalized group of worshipers.

In my daily conversations with God, I recognized the evil nature of and guilt associated with sin and the joy of repentance and forgiveness. I always realized my Creator was unconditionally on my side—Protector, Provider, Defender, at all times loving and looking out for my welfare.

I engaged my God in lengthy dialogues, feeling a font of strength rise within as I came to know Him more deeply. He spoke to me through an inner voice, telling me it was now my time to live the kind of life I wanted, if I was willing to make the right decisions.

I soon discovered that the more faith I put in God, the more powerful His messages became. "You are not to be a victim," God said to me, "and you are not going to be victimized by the past."

Empowered by my spiritual relationship, I felt indomitable. No longer feeling sorry for myself, I moved forward accepting responsibility for the choices and decisions I made. *Someone* cared about me now, *Someone who* I could trust and who reciprocated my trust uncompromisingly.

Just eighteen months after leaving Marilyn's guardianship, I went from believing she and the other parishioners who attended Sunday service were wacky with their talk of baptism and biblical teachings, to recognizing the Holy Spirit had enlightened me! I had been granted more than a blessing—I received a miracle.

Even though I had not yet been baptized, I felt infused with the grace I needed to pursue my new journey. Not quite eighteen, after my experiences with over ten foster care families of diverse or no beliefs, I was puzzled by the plethora of religions and spiritual paths I could follow.

Yearning to be baptized, I realized it was now time to get the spiritual education necessary in order to make the best decision possible. Determined to make the right choice, I visited different churches and spent time in silence, in reflection and in dialogue with God, certain He would whisper where He wanted me to go.

One day, after having lunch with my grandmother Donna, we drove past a quaint mission church. Although it was neither large nor grandiose, the grounds were beautiful, lush and a bright emerald green. "Grandma," I said as we neared, "we have driven past this old mission so many times, but I have never been inside. Can we go in and look around?"

"I know the priests who live there," she said, "let's go in for a tour. I'm certain they will be happy to have some visitors."

We parked the car and went inside. I was immediately captured by the atmosphere of stillness and a faint aroma of incense. On the walls hung pictures of various men and women, some dressed in long dark robes. There were also several statues and rows of red candles, some lit and others not, in front of the icons.

We slipped into one of the wooden pews and sat. It creaked, but reverently, almost fearful of disturbing the hallowed aura. Fascinated by the stillness and simplistic beauty, I turned my head in continuation trying to absorb my surroundings.

Although the mission was in darkness, a ray of mid-afternoon sun penetrating a stained glass window cast a beam of light across the altar, illuminating a silver crucifix placed in the center. A small pottery vase filled with multi-colored wild garden-picked flowers stood on the left side next to a large closed book. On either side were two, foot-long white candles in metal holders—unlit.

It was so quiet and so reverent. Time became a nonexistent factor, and I have no idea how long we sat there listening to our own thoughts. "God," I whispered, "are you here? Where are you?" I repeated my questions over and over, calmly, then pleading in a more demanding tone.

I felt a magnetic surge of energy—at first baffling, as most unknowns. Like a cadence in crescendo, it climbed until it climaxed into an almost delirious aura of inner serenity. The confusion in my mind, the unrest living in my soul for years all seemed to have evaporated.

An ever present sensation of heaviness lifted. I closed my eyes and took a long, steady breath. The hollow void seemed less pronounced. Furthermore, I felt a strong presence beside me—it seemed as if someone was enclosing me in a firm, but gentle embrace.

Suddenly the words of Mary Stevenson's Poem, *Footprints in the Sand*, sprang into my mind. Not recalling when I had read it, I recognized God's influence in my time of distress. It was His way of reassuring me that I was no longer alone. I whispered the part of the poem closest to my heart, feeling a wave of calm rush through the anxiety and fear.

"Lord, You said that once I decided to follow you, You'd walk with me all the way. But I have noticed that during the most troublesome times in my life, there is only one set of footprints. I don't understand why when I needed you most you would leave me." The Lord replied, "My son, My precious child, I love you and I would never leave you. During your times of trial and suffering, when you see only one set of footprints, it was then that I Carried You."

Drenched in the ecstasy of enlightenment, I knew I had found my spiritual identity—God was 'carrying' me to the Roman Catholic Church.

Released from the questioning and doubts, moments after I walked into the Old Spanish Mission Church on Mission Avenue in San Diego, I was grounded for the first time in my life. Certainly not a foster care revolving door experience, I knew this was for keeps.

A short, stocky, Friar dressed in a long brown robe tapped me on the shoulder after greeting my grandmother. Caught by surprise I jumped, leaving behind my reflections. He seemed like a jovial soul with his round face and kind eyes. My grandmother exchanged a few words with him, probably explaining our visit. Then gently nudging him on the arm, she introduced us.

"Take your time," he whispered softly with a pronounced Spanish accent. "If you have any questions please let me know. I'm either here in the church or over at the rectory." I was moved by his graciousness and the sweetness of his personality. He seemed at peace and so willing to be of assistance.

I thanked him, returning my attention to the Lord, who had drawn me into the old Spanish Mission Church. Sometimes I questioned if this was always my path, only God forgot to lead me to it.

It was about a new relationship with *Someone* who loved me regardless of my past, *Someone* willing to forgive yesterday's deeds as human failings. I was right in the eye of the storm—protected by a new calmness and stillness, feeling the outpouring of grace. I found God. And once I embraced my Creator, my faith was ever present and unwavering.

My outlook changed. For the first time I realized that I had a purpose—I was born for a reason. A sudden wisdom seemed to have descended upon me. Reflecting, I began to understand the meaning of my suffering. All the misery, tears and anguish were not wasted experiences. But, was I asked to bear torments and troubles for a greater good—even though I was not yet able to decipher this good?

I began to wonder about the strong bond I was forming with God and the message He was sending me. Certainly, I had a mission, but the 'what when and how' were still unknowns. Perhaps even today, decades later, I cannot define this purpose. But the realization that I did have a 'reason to be' turned my life around in many significant ways. I had the certainty God is a constant presence in my life, and I'm now 'asked' to make a difference in the lives of others. Perhaps the inspiration for this book is part of my reason to be. Perhaps I'm a disciple of Christ, treading the thorny paths to introduce God to others.

While still living with Tammy and Gary, I had begun a 'prayer list.' Feeling as if it was time to turn my life around and move away from the distressing foster care circuit, I asked God to come rescue me. It was the number one priority on my list. 'Please allow me to return home and begin my life,' I wrote. My prayer was granted.

Since I lacked the spiritual savvy to understand the benevolent, forgiving nature of God, I did not realize that pleadings for ill or evil fates to befall others would not be granted. Consequently, I wrote a prayer begging God to absent Uncle George from my life. 'I don't ever want to see, speak or hear from him again,' I put on my prayer list. Basically, I wanted him dead! Of course this intention was not granted.

Wonderful as my enlightenment was, my conversion did not transform me overnight. Still dysfunctional, I had a long path to follow before I could purge the hate and evil thoughts from my heart and become a true Christian.

The terrible nightmares returned with a vengeance, leaving me saturated in perspiration, shuddering in fright and unable to return to sleep, night after night. Realizing my need for Divine Intervention, I asked God to remove these horrendous 'happenings' from my life.

Petrified of tripping and falling down the hollow staircase after the ghosts had haunted me again, seeding unrest in my days, I added to my prayer list a request to relocate from the present house. In a postscript, I thanked God for my faith and the hope it instilled in me. It was, at this time, all I had.

I returned home to a new situation. Uncle George was gone, though not deceased as I had wanted, and my mother appeared to be more in control of her wild mood swings and crippling bouts of depression. She and Cindy had bonded, and I noticed, were often planning fun activities together like ice skating and snow-ski vacations.

Envy swelling within, I realized this was the life I had always coveted. Instead of feeling happy for the transformation, I felt alone and more abandoned—cheated as the first-born daughter who had been unjustly scorned and extradited from the family.

Then God came to my rescue. He opened my eyes, showing me how to recognize and share the joy of others. Gradually, my feelings of jealousy and resentment melted into a serene acceptance of the situation. Eventually, I allowed their happiness to touch my heart. I stepped away from the bittersweet rancor of witnessing them in sync with each other and began to share their contentment.

At just a few weeks shy of age eighteen, it was time to be self-sufficient, a concept that equated to getting a driver's license and seeking employment. Although I was living at home, I had to be financially responsible for my clothing and the maintenance, eventually, of a car. This meant I had to learn how to drive.

In my opinion, Dawn Hammond, a good friend of my mother's, demonstrated extraordinary courage when she volunteered to accept the role of driving instructor. A slender, attractive twenty-four-year-old woman with a sparkling, outgoing personality, long dark hair and big brown, friendly eyes, she took me under her wing as a big sister.

Throughout the foster care, Juvenile Hall, South Wood Mental Health Facility and Juvenile Crisis Resolution Program experiences, she reassured me that my mother was distraught, missed my presence in her life and was trying to find a solution to remedy the situation.

I was caught off-guard by Dawn's revelation. Much as I wanted to believe my mom loved me, I slammed my foot on the emotional brake, unwilling to accept as true what I was still dubious about.

Certainly, her behavior all those years, governed by a far too permissive outlook regarding Uncle George's brutality in my regard, did not demonstrate a loving maternal heart. I was neither protected nor defended during the vicious beatings.

Consequently, she would have to do a great deal more than confide a few comments to Dawn if she wanted to win my trust—if, in effect, it was possible at this point in my life. I was seriously wounded and the scarring was painfully deep.

Despite the irresolvable conflicts, I felt a new inner happiness. I had found God and I was at home. For the first time in my life, I dared to hope.

Dawn took me out on the road and introduced me to her husband, Larry. Tall, dark and handsome, with amazing eyes that spoke of his kindhearted, unassuming manner, he was a man who loved, adored and cherished his wife. Captivated, I was knocked off my feet. With a 'young girl live happily ever after prince charming' view of life, I thought he was truly the perfect man to carry me off into the sunset.

"Wow," I said to myself, "what a man! This is what marriage is all about. I must pray and ask God to bring me a Larry of my own when I am ready to settle down."

I was certain that having a good looking man who loved and appreciated me would be the answer to all my prayers. Having received a second chance, I wanted to make the best of it. Though I was still far too young to make life-long commitments, I realized I had to decide the path I wanted to follow, set objectives and devise a plan in order to turn my intentions into reality.

I also realized I would need the help of God if I wanted to succeed. Prayer would be my means to attaining all that I wanted, and I prayed daily asking for what I perceived as 'a normal life.' Recognizing the power of God, I was sure He could understand what was in my mind and heart.

What mattered was that I had my prayer list and God was granting me my wishes. Mom and Uncle George had divorced, removing an impediment prohibiting her from gaining visitation rights. I kept 'writing' my wishes on my prayer list and checking off the favors granted. God was listening to me—He was really there—and He cared!

Dawn proved to be an excellent instructor. She had patience and was fearless enough to climb into a vehicle with an inexperienced teen. On the other hand, after several lessons and some practice runs, I was sure of myself, took the driving exam, passed and was awarded my license.

Once I had accomplished this task, I applied for and obtained a job with a new start-up business, owned by Jim and Nancy, *The California Yogurt Company*. A wealthy couple, they lived in a luxurious home and were able to give their children beautiful clothes and new cars when they turned sixteen. Blessed with material benefits and a sense of serenity, I considered them an ideal family.

Unbeknown to me, Jim and Nancy were fully aware of my tormented past—every foster care interlude and all the institutional 'vacations' in between. Yet, trusting my ability to handle the business despite a much sought after resume, they offered me a full time position to organize and run their first store. This gave them the freedom to research additional locations for a future business plan expansion.

Welcomed into the family, I felt comfortable with their son and daughter, building a warm, friendly relationship. For the first time in my life I was accepted, deemed a capable person and entrusted with serious responsibilities. My life had made a one hundred and eighty degree pirouette from being shunned as incorrigible to being accountable. Filled with aspirations and interesting challenges, I had a reason to awaken each morning and retired every evening feeling satisfied with my day's accomplishments. The new path, upon which I journeyed, seemed smooth and uncluttered under my footsteps.

I guess it was difficult to shake my dysfunctional nature and the devastating effects of the previous decade of terror. I had faith and I prayed, but after the transgression of Adam and Eve, mankind was known as a species of sinners. And sadly, I was no different.

Several employees, most of them high school seniors, and myself included fell prey to the temptation to 'help' ourselves to an extra $20.00 every day. Foolishly believing it was an easy to commit and get away with crime, we stole the money right from the register, then darted next door to the discount shoe outlet and exchanged it for a pair of new shoes.

Unfortunately, not yet morally and ethically liable, I did not fully comprehend the consequences and implications of my actions. And unable to grasp the harm I was doing, I actually thought a few missing $20.00 bills a day would not have an influence on Jim and Nancy's business. Egoistically, I focused on the fact that justice was being served—I was finally getting the new shoes I deserved, but was unable to afford until now.

Unaware I was trying to justify a serious wrongdoing, I never paused to consider how my selfishness would eventually deprive me of a blessing God had granted and cause distress and disappointment in a family that had so benevolently befriended me.

It didn't take a Nobel Prize wining mathematician to discover the theft. Chosen as the 'guinea pig' because it was known among all the employees that I was Jim and Nancy's favorite, they felt I would get off easier. With the fingers pointed in my direction, Jim and Nancy filled out a robbery report and I was arrested.

I was at work as usual, clueless the crime had been discovered. Two policemen entered and I was certain their intent was to buy yogurt. "May I help you," I said smiling, eager to serve and make a sale.

"Are you Margaret?" a tall, stern-looking officer blurted, fixing his gaze on mine. I felt a shudder run though my body. "Yes," I responded, almost choking on my saliva. With the icy chill came the realization something was very wrong. Just as I responded the second officer roughly grabbed my arms, pulled them behind my back and clipped on a pair of cold metal handcuffs.

"Margaret," he said, "you are under arrest for robbery." Then I heard what sounded like, "You have the right to remain silent." Petrified, I realized I was being apprehended and given into the custody of the two officers.

Escorted to the police vehicle parked outside, I was seated in the rear and locked in. At the station I was read the Miranda Warning which I didn't quite understand except for, "You have the right to remain silent. Anything you say can be used against you in a court of law." All the rest was Greek.

How foolish I was, I thought to myself. I had been given a chance for a new life, and for sheer greed I threw it all to the wind. Here I was back in jail. But this time, unlike it the past, I was not a victim of circumstance, but a culprit caught stealing. I was guilty of committing a crime.

Divested of my possessions, I was photographed, fingerprinted and locked in a cell. Recognizing how hard I had struggled to be accepted and treated as a normal individual, I had failed to realize the gravity of my actions, how disappointed Jim and Nancy were and how much this family loved and cared about me.

I was totally incapable of 'love definition, recognition and appreciation.' I neither felt it nor appreciated it. Instead I was apathetic to it, never having truly experienced it. As a survivor, I believed that whatever happened, happened. All I could do was collect the pieces and continue along my journey.

At first I did not recognize the arresting officer as the policeman who had taken me to Juvenile Hall earlier in my life, and I believe he didn't make the connection either. Now, unlike the previous time, I turned to God. Visualizing my prayer list I mentally added a plea for forgiveness. "Please God," I begged, my eyes swelling with tears, "what have I done! I'm so very sorry. Can you forgive me? Please don't let Jim and Nancy press charges. I know I have done wrong and I promise I will never take something that doesn't belong to me ever again."

I repeated this imploration over and over, begging for clemency. Never had I felt such remorse and guilt for something I had done. My regret and repentance surprised me. Aware I was now accountable, I realized I had to make amends, lift myself from the fall, climb out of the hole and move on.

I spoke openly and truthfully with the police officer, confessing my crime. Thankfully, he was compassionate toward me once he recognized me and called to mind my prior experiences and despondent family history.

"Could you please help me?" I asked, begging for his intervention. "I regret what I did and I want to make this right."

Releasing me from my cell, he accompanied me to his office to explain and complete the booking process.

"Margaret," he said, sighing, "growing up was not easy for me either. Like you, I had an awful childhood filled with abuse and neglect. I was in many different foster homes and never had any stability or anyone who really cared about me."

His eyes moistened as he spoke and I could see he was visibly moved by reliving some of those ghastly experiences. Clearing his throat he said, "You control your own destiny. If you want to change your life and make a difference, you must do it yourself. No one can do it for you." I listened since he had not allowed his early years to determine the rest of his life. Instead, he had overcome his demons, turned himself around and made something of his life.

"How can I get myself out of this?" I asked.

"Margaret," he responded, patting me on the hand, "you can start by telling the truth."

He then advised me to write an apology letter to Jim and Nancy asking them not to press charges against me and promised he would personally intervene on my behalf and ask them to reconsider their position.

"I won't send you back to the cell," he said, "just sit here a minute, think about what you did, and write the letter."

I knew this was God answering my prayer. He had sent me a guardian angel!

I followed his advice and expressed my regret and sorrow to Nancy and Jim. Upon reading my letter, he reassured me he believed I was telling the truth.

Several hours later I was released from custody. When my mother arrived, the officer stood by my side.

"Margaret realizes she has made a terrible mistake," he announced, immediately coming to my defense. "She understands the consequences attached to such bad actions. I feel confident she has learned a lesson, and it will never happen again."

My God-sent 'guardian angel' knew exactly what I was up against. Having walked along the same path, he was fully aware of the challenges I had to face and how difficult it would be to reconcile with my mother. But he tried, and I was warmed by his empathy and enlightened by God's intervention—He answered my prayers.

Once in the car my mother looked directly ahead as if concentrating on the traffic. Although she had turned her life around and no longer erupted in angry outbursts, shouting insulting remarks, I could see she was anxious. At the first red light she blurted through pursed lips, "I was wondering how long your good behavior would last. I guess it was just too much to expect from you."

Apparently the officer had not succeeded in convincing her I was repentant and focused on changing my life.

Every word she said—every angry breath she took—every sneering look she gave me, served no purpose but to seed more hatred in my heart.

The skeptic was not exclusively my mother. The officer did not have an easy time trying to convince Jim and Nancy to drop the charges. They were furious with me and adamant about following through with their accusations. His only loophole was to explain my background and give them a bit of my family history.

Although Jim and Nancy eventually accepted my apology, they disassociated themselves from me. I was cut out of their lives and instructed never to step foot in any of their yogurt shops now and in the near future—a sentence far more painful than any jail time. I forfeited the love and respect of the only people who were willing to care about me.

My friends soon discovered what I had done and for several months I was the talk of the town. But I moved on and honored their request not return to their shop. Whenever I drove by to pick up my friends who were employed there, I would wait in the car, feeling regretful for my foolish mistake.

Upset and disappointed for having hurt the wonderful people who trusted me, I discovered I actually had a conscience—for the first time in my life I was bothered by the idea of harming someone! Not only did I have a sense of right and wrong, but I had scruples. Undoubtedly, this was the work of God, remolding me.

Even though I committed a serious wrong, I felt as if blood was running through my veins. I was a human being, a person willing to step out of the shadows, admit my error and take full responsibility for my deeds. What a powerful turnaround! What an empowering learning experience!

Although at the time I did not have the faintest inclination that what comes around goes around, ultimately this incident would return later in life.

Eventually my mother came to realize I was genuinely repentant for my evil actions. "Margaret, I believe you are truly sorry for stealing from Jim and Nancy," she said one day, "and I don't think you were the ringleader. Maybe you just went along with the others."

Her words uplifted my spirit. I felt lighthearted. Was it possible I actually cared what my mother thought? Did her vote of confidence really mean something to me?

I tried to get back into the rhythm of life by getting another job and spending time with my friends. As an attractive young girl, I was never without a young man asking me for a date. However, at this point in my life I was neither willing nor able to undertake a relationship.

Burdened with insurmountable trust issues, I could not deal with conflicts and disagreements. Furthermore, I was emotionally volatile. My feelings had a rather abbreviated life span. Maybe it was a form of undiagnosed EDD, emotional deficit disorder! One day I was out with them, the next day they were history—unrecorded history.

My friends started talking about marriage—meeting a nice guy preferably with money, settling down and having a family. My thoughts and wishes could not have been further apart from theirs. But I just had absolutely no feelings for men.

As soon as I was recuperated from my 'brush with the law,' I got another full-time job. My relationship with my family was still in the reparatory stages, and my tormenting nightmares continued to interrupt my sleep. Sadly, I was not successful in bonding with either my mother or Cindy, but we were on friendly terms, extending courtesies and acts of kindness when warranted.

Most of my leisure time was dedicated to my grand-mother Donna and trying to decipher where I wanted to go from here; what I wanted and expected from life, and how I was going to accomplish my objectives.

"Margaret, you are a young attractive woman," my grandmother told me, offering what she thought was excellent advice, "you should seriously find an older man who is able to take care of you."

Grandmother Donna spoke frankly, believing this was the best long-term solution for my life. However, she was unaware I had many dates and proposals complete with eye-dazzling engagement rings, but no interest to pursue them.

I was incapable of love, which made marriage an out of the question, almost ridiculous life choice. Recognizing my friends were dealing with romantic aches and pains, 'traumatic' break-ups and a behind the back playing the field infidelity, I promised myself I was not going down that street. Furthermore, I would be certain to protect myself from the heartaches my friends were bearing.

Piece by piece, I constructed and hid behind the largest shield imaginable, growing more distant and hardened towards men. Puzzled by the emotional death, I did not understand the workings of this psychological defense mechanism until much later—after years of introspection and groping in the dark crevices of my being.

Unwilling to confront this demon, I pushed it out of my mind, opting to move forward without ever glancing back. If I didn't dwell on it—if I didn't visualize it—it would not exist!

Chapter 8

Deliverance Due to the Grace of God

"O Lord, how many are my adversaries! Many
rise up against me! Many are saying of me,
'There is no salvation from him in God.'
But you, O Lord, are my shield; my glory,
you lift up my head!"
—Psalm3:2-4

Despite my failings and the constant frustration of persistent demons returning to torment me, I knew God had other plans. Realizing it was time to assume full responsibility for my life and be accountable financially for my well-being, I continued to pray for wisdom and the strength to follow the right path.

After the serious *California Yogurt Company* fiasco, I learned to appreciate my blessings and not squander the kindness of others in pursuit of greed. I was trusted, respected for my capabilities and put in a position with potential to grow. Foolishly, I did not evaluate the opportunity that had opened up in front of me nor the people who had believed in me.

However, I did learn a valuable life lesson—if someone had faith in me, perhaps I should be more willing to explore my possibilities. Maybe I was not just an incorrigible girl, good for nothing and without a future. I decided to give it serious consideration.

My first project was to find myself a full-time job. Without a high school diploma I did not have the credentials to gain status as a good candidate for employment. However, so far nothing was ever easy for me, and although the road was filled with hurdles, I had to admit I was moving along.

Checking the classifieds, I noticed an insert advertising a position for a service writer at a car wash not too distant from where I lived.

Invoking the name of God for assistance, I presented myself, and expressed an interest in the job. Because of the excellent compensation structure, the service writer position was a magnet attracting endless individuals seeking a relatively lucrative career opportunity. Since the car wash was a high volume, multi-million dollar operation, the position earned a moderate base salary plus substantial commissions.

I met the manager who willingly interviewed and hired me on the spot. Apparently, God was in accord with my choice. Undoubtedly, I was in the right place at the right time.

As a service writer, I was on my feet most of the day, guiding the vehicles through the service process. When cars pulled in I'd inquire about their requests and write the tickets for the different services. The money was wonderful. Suddenly, I found myself elevated from a mere minimum-wage earner struggling to survive to a position where I was bringing home $400 or $500 a week. I was certain I had struck gold. This was my chance for independence. At nineteen years of age, I was now able to support myself.

In addition to individuals, I also handled big corporate accounts. One client, Miller Distribution, brought in all their service and private vehicles: a business deal that changed my life.

John was the twenty-seven-year-old grandson of the founder of Miller Distribution. A wealthy young man of German decent, he was short and robust of constitution. His ruddy complexion was framed with sandy blonde hair and accentuated by blue eyes.

Though not particularly handsome in a Hollywood sense, John had the imposing, overly confident demeanor of a successful professional. Arrogant and authoritarian, he made certain his presence was noted.

John was a man who had been born with a silver spoon in his mouth. Experiencing neither poverty nor deprivation, he grew up in a culture that glorifies materialism and abundance.

Accustomed to getting everything he wanted, and wanting everything he laid his eyes on, he set his sights on capturing me, never anticipating my unintentional 'hard to get' strategy. His wealth and elevated social status earned him the most sought after 'good catch' label, and he was well aware of his attractive position in the world of young women of marriage age.

However, not interested in pursuing John's advances, I snubbed his romantic attentions and invitations. Still not interested in men, I just didn't feel any 'chemistry.' Both my mother and grandmother knew him, and I was repeatedly chastised for refusing his dinner invitations.

"John is such a nice man, Margaret," they would say, "he's from a good family, he's rich and he can take care of you. Why don't you go out with him?"

What could we possibly have in common, I asked myself repeatedly? Somehow intrigued by our differences, I decided to give it a try.

Several months later, John arrived to pick me up for an early date. After greeting my mom and Cindy, he took me gently by the arm and led me out the front door.

"It's all yours, Margaret," he said pointing to a brand new 1985 silver Mazda RX 7, one of the year's most popular sports cars. Relaxing his grip from my arm, he dug into his trouser pocket and pulled out a shiny silver key chain with two keys dangling.

Lifting my hand he pressed it into my palm. "This is for you," he said, brimming with self-confidence. "What do you think? Do you like it? Why don't you just drive around in it!"

Feeling neither excitement nor interest, I didn't even bother to feign enthusiasm. I just didn't care much about the car or even about John. A generous soul who believed in going all out, he brought presents for my mom and family whenever he came to visit. Presumably, the extravagant gift giving was his way of wooing and trying to entice me into falling in love with him.

However, I was not romantically involved. Although he courted me in grand style, there were no ripples of passion—no sweaty palms, loss of concentration and or appetite, and no sleepless nights with love-induced palpitations. John was a good friend and nothing more, a well educated young man offering a promising future. I enjoyed his company even without the sizzles of passion. I liked his very special attentions. It was certainly a welcome change to have someone actually care about me!

John and I soon became an 'item.' Enjoying a whirl-wind extravaganza of fun, sailing on his boat and jet skiing, I was hounded by family and friends encouraging me to seriously consider John as a life partner.

When I introduced John to Stephanie, one of my school friends, she was adamant about my continuing to date him. "Margaret," she blurted, "this is what you need. He's a perfect catch and he likes you! He's crazy about you—everyone can see that!"

Most probably, I pursued getting to know John not only as a result of the incessant pressure I received from family and peers, but because I was drawn to his big, solid, close-knit family—something I never had but always coveted. It was almost an obsession. Often I would date or befriend individuals from nice families just to be accepted and considered part of a world so unknown to me.

John had found out that my mother had decided to relocate and was moving to another state to pursue a better employment option. It was her first attempt to gain total independence.

"Don't worry, Margaret," John said reassuringly, "I'll take care of you after she's gone."

Realizing he was moving in the direction of a stroll down the aisle to the altar, and recognizing my own aversion to marriage at nineteen, I began distancing myself. In my heart I knew it was over—John and I were traveling in opposite directions.

Shortly thereafter, I decided to end my relationship with one of the 'best catches' in the neighborhood. Upset with my 'rash' decision, my mother was beyond furious. "That's the best you'll ever get," she snarled through pursed lips. "How could you make such a foolish mistake? You better think it over carefully before you tell him!"

Discrediting everything about my mother, I neither valued her opinions nor trusted her motives. Consequently, I questioned and contested whatever advice or admonition she so generously threw at me and took the opposite path.

John was a nice gentleman, but I was not in love with him. I knew there was no way I would sell my soul and take a man as my husband exclusively for financial gain. It did not matter that I was brutally criticized for my decision. My self-respect was more important and I was ready to continue along my journey without John. I had planned to tell him after our next date.

I continued working at the car wash, repeatedly asking God to help me deal with and overcome my daily trials. Believing the stress from my work was the culprit for my queasy, uneasy stomach, I mentioned to my mother that I had been feeling sick for several months. Immediately, she phoned the doctor and scheduled a checkup. I didn't mention anything to John as I was sure everything would eventually be OK, and the ill feelings would disappear as they had appeared. I was convinced I had probably caught some nasty bug.

After a sonogram of my abdomen, the doctor said, "Margaret, I don't have to do any tests. I can hear a heartbeat—you are pregnant—that's why you have been feeling nauseous. The baby is healthy and the pregnancy is moving along smoothly."

The room spun around: "pregnant" I repeated over and over in my mind. "I'm pregnant!" Shocked, I felt lightheaded, as if I was about to faint. This was not in my plan. I was not going to marry and have a family. It could not be happening to me!

"You're just about sixteen weeks along," the doctor said, interrupting my thoughts, gazing at the monitor. I turned as he pointed to a confusing pulsating image. Squinting to focus better, I noticed it suddenly took on the semblance of a tiny disproportionate embryo with an oversized head. It seemed to be floating.

"How could this be?" I questioned. "My cycle has been normal. I never skipped a period."

"It's not common," he replied, "but it can occur."

"Nothing about me is normal," I blurted. "After all, I've always been dysfunctional."

"Now, Margaret," he said, clearing his throat, "you will have to make a decision immediately—either to have an abortion or keep it."

"Abortion is out of the question," I shrieked. "I can hear the heartbeat—I can see it on the screen—it's a baby! Who would kill an innocent baby?" Abortion was never an option for me—it didn't even cross my mind. Years later thinking back, I realize how easy, perhaps, it would have been to end it all, yet how powerful the influence of God was in determining my fate. He had certainly taken the reins and was directing my life.

My mother, in agreement with my decision and almost delirious about the birth of her first grandchild, suddenly took on a supportive role.

Ready to depart for her new job, she was leaving me and my sister alone to fend for ourselves, at respectively nineteen and seventeen years of age. Promising to assume financial responsibility for the maintenance of the house, she made it clear that food, non-edible provisions, and other incidentals of life were our obligation.

Although in the midst of a divorce, when Uncle George came to the house, my mother told him about my pregnancy. Saddened by her news, he was concerned I was wearing the jeans to conceal my condition. "Margaret," he said, "take off those jeans, you're suffocating the baby!" Shocked by his concern, I responded by absenting myself from the room. Obviously, the jeans were still a safe, comfortable fit or I would not have been wearing them. Despite my young age, there was no way I would ever jeopardize the well-being of my baby.

The time had come for me to confront John about my decision to break off our relationship. Realizing my pregnancy was now obvious, I knew I could no longer conceal the truth.

I was still working at the car wash as a service writer and a bit concerned about supporting myself and my baby. What was once a seemingly good salary now seemed a doubtful one. Would I be able to make it?

As my pregnancy advanced, I convinced myself God had implanted this baby in my womb as a special gift. He wanted me to bring a new life into the world—it was in keeping with His plan for me.

Expressing my feeling freely earned me sarcastic snickers and mocking whispers questioning my sanity. However, regardless of the condescending gossip, I chose to believe in Divine Intervention, accepting the birth of my baby as a means to change my life for the better. My child would be my salvation.

Eventually, John noticed my considerable weight gain, all localized in one specific area. A frequent client at the car wash, there was no way I could have avoided meeting him. "Margaret," he said eyeing my middle, "you're pregnant!" Of course denying it would not have been even minimally credible.

Although I had concocted a story with a good friend of mine at work, Nicky, to conveniently point a finger in his direction, thus transferring paternity away from John, he did not go for it. "The baby is mine," he said patting my stomach. "I know that's my child."

Nicky was a wonderful friend who would do almost anything for me. Hailing from a Japanese mother and Black Japanese father, he had a rather exotic and interesting look with a pair of dark almond eyes and a head full of thick black hair. Together, we were quite a conspicuous couple.

Nicky and I flew off to Las Vegas, unlike star-crossed lovers enveloped in passion, eloping at dusk, to say our "I dos." This last minute scenario was orchestrated to resolve my pregnancy situation and remove some of my concerns regarding John's threat to take my baby away. How naive I was.

We went ahead with the wedding. Uncle George failed to appear, but my mother did attend the ceremony.

When John found out Nicky had slipped a ring on my finger, he was infuriated. "You're having my baby," John sneered, approaching Nicky at the car wash. "How will you feel raising my son or daughter?" It seemed like a scene from one of the daytime talk shows.

"God help me," I prayed in the evenings, scared to death of a future I could neither manage nor manipulate. Sweating and breathless from an unforgiving anxiety, I'd implore the mercy of God.

"Please God, help me resolve this situation. I promise this will be the last time I'll have to beg for *Your* intervention." I repeated my pray over and over, dubious my decision to coerce Nicky into marrying me was really the answer.

We moved back into my mother's house and awaited the birth. Life with Nicky was far from ideal, and certainly a long way from happy. Recognizing I had made a serious error in marrying Nicky, I knew I had to concentrate on bringing a healthy baby into the world—it was my priority. All else would have to wait, and eventually, with the help of God I would resolve my issues.

In keeping with my lifestyle to date, my daughter Chalice's birth represented another major hurdle to overcome. However, the challenging turn of events did not catch me off-guard—simply because I did not expect an easy time. After all, nothing was ever without complexity or complications, so why should this be any different?

Several weeks prior to my due date, my physician informed me that at barely five feet tall, my petite constitution and pelvic bones would not consent to a smooth, natural birth.

"Margaret," he said, checking the ultrasound; "it's really doubtful that you can deliver naturally. I fear the baby's head is far too large for your narrow birth canal. We will have to perform a C-section to assure your safety as well as the baby's."

"I'd really prefer to have the baby naturally," I blurted, intentioned to fully experience the birth of my daughter at all costs. Too naïve and inexperienced to understand what I was up against, I insisted, discounting the advice and recommendation of a professional who had brought hundreds of children into the world. Denying the risks I was foolishly taking for myself and my baby, I refused to give birth by Caesarean Section. I just wouldn't hear of it.

Having passed my due date by several weeks, the doctor was concerned the baby was growing even larger, which would further complicate the birth, thus increasing the risks. "Margaret, you're overdue and the contractions have not yet started. We have to induce labor," the doctor announced during my tenth month visit. "I'm worried about complications, plus in a post-term pregnancy there could be a possibility your placenta may no longer provide sufficient nutrients to the baby."

I chose September fourth since in 1986 it fell on Labor Day, and I felt it would be a most fitting day to deliver. Smiling, I arrived at the hospital at seven AM. Nicky accompanied me, behaving as any 'father' awaiting the birth of his first child.

With the name of God on my lips and a prayer in my heart, I watched as the nurse inserted the slender IV needle in my hand. Too excited to feel the pinch of my pierced skin, I didn't even flinch. After an examination revealed my cervix was ready, a combination of hormones and a relaxant was pumped into my veins to stimulate uterine contractions.

The prayers continued. Poor God—I was being a real pest that day—but I was also carrying out His wishes by bringing one of His creatures into the world. Within a few hours I had dilated only to four centimeters. Concerned the contractions were not coming fast enough, the doctor ordered a more potent drug cocktail for the IV.

This time the drip worked and in a short time I was painfully dilated to seven centimeters. At one minute intervals, the contractions were excruciatingly agonizing, leaving me on the brink of literally passing out. I cried out for something to lessen if not alleviate my pain.

Glancing at the fetal monitor the doctor discovered that the intensity of my pain had peaked beyond the highest level. "She's in hard labor," he said. "The drug accelerated the contractions too soon. I cannot administer any pain medication without potentially harming the baby."

Trying to catch my breath, I was unable to speak. The piercing intermittent pain was nothing I would have ever predicted. It felt as if my insides were being twisted and brutally ripped out.

"This is great," I thought to myself. "It must be pay back time—this has to be some type of punishment." Delirious from the pain, I pushed and prayed for the next ten hours, trying to deliver my baby.

It was at this point that I had an out-of-body experience. Feeling as if I was suctioned from my body, I felt an uncanny sensation of floating and hovering above myself.

Several minutes later my limbs went numb. I couldn't feel my arms or legs. My tongue seemed paralyzed leaving me incapable of uttering a word.

I noticed my mother and grandmother, huddled together in a corner of the room. From the rhythmic heaving of their shoulders, I knew they were crying. Why didn't I feel any pain? I interpreted my sudden, almost beatific state as a sign I was near death. *But why would God take me now?* I questioned. *I have too much to do.*

"Margaret, we no longer hear the baby's heart beat," the doctor said, interrupting my dream-like state. "Stop pushing!"

Get the straps," he continued, "then come here and wipe my forehead." I could see he was sweating profusely. As the nurse reached for the thick leather straps, I felt a hand gently caress my shoulder.

"Margaret, I'm sorry, but we have to strap you down to prohibit you from giving in to the urge to push. In the meantime we'll prepare you for an emergency Caesarean delivery! Since we cannot hear the baby's heartbeat, I have summoned a specialist from the fetal-neonatal neurology department. As soon as she gets here and completes an evaluation of the situation, we can proceed with the C-section."

'Strap me down—leather straps.' His words brought me crashing back to reality. Reentering my body was exasperating. Agonizingly insufferable, the pain jolted my mind into flashback mode. An uncensored panorama of my days at South Wood Mental Health Facility sprang before my eyes. The sights, sounds, smells, lights and darkness intensified as I visualized screaming, kicking teens and children being violently subdued, strapped down with thick leather bands.

Confused, I wondered what kind of labor I was in that would warrant leather shackles. Was I in a hospital? Why was I undergoing such torment to have a baby? Grief-stricken, I knew I had to speak up and defend myself before I would be tortured to death.

But the words did not come out. With difficulty I tried to catch my breath and let out a scream—again I heard just the raspy sound of my own silence.

After what seemed like an endless amount of time, I was introduced to the anesthesiologist. *Could it be possible,* I thought to myself, *that finally after the agony someone was actually providing a pain-alleviating solution?*

I prayed to God comparing my pain to the Crucifixion. If Jesus could suffer excruciating agony for three hours, I guess I could bear this cross: but I whispered—God I need your help.

And God heard my prayer—"I'm going to put you completely under," the anesthesiologist said. "We have to get the baby out as quickly as possible. But I want to warn you," he continued, smiling as he took my hand, "you may feel as if you are dying since the pain will disappear. Don't worry, I will be here with you all through the delivery, until you awaken."

"Thank you, God," I whispered, seconds before I went under!

I was out for about twelve hours, and when I opened my eyes I was told I had given birth to a beautiful baby girl whom I had named Chalice. Eager to meet my daughter I asked to see her right away.

Obliging my anxious new mother requests, the nurse carried Chalice in and gently laid her in a crib at the foot of my bed. "This is your beautiful Chalice," the nurse said, smiling. "Isn't she just precious?" I glanced at her sweet round face, framed by a mass of long dark hair. Yes—she certainly was a beauty. Undoubtedly, God had given me a very special gift.

Chalice seemed so peaceful, lying there staring at me with her huge blue eyes. In return I stared back, not really sure what I should do or say. It was obvious I was new at this and not very well-informed.

There was an almost hallowed stillness in the room as mother and daughter exchanged their first glances in total silence. "Lord," I said, "what am I going to do with Chalice? How will I care for her and tend to her needs when I am barely capable of caring for myself?"

I prayed to God because I knew in my heart He was there for me and would assist me along my journey. After many years of spiritual darkness, I had walked into the Divine light. And all it took was meeting, accepting and getting to know my Creator. Now we had a powerful relationship. Looking back, I often wondered how I was able to survive without Him.

Chalice was a perfect baby. She neither cried nor fussed as most newborns have a tendency to do. Instead, she just lay still most of the time staring up at me. Actually I sometimes fantasized she was asking God, "Why have you given me this 'child' as my mother?"

Meanwhile, Nicky's mother came to visit her grand-daughter. Leaning over the crib she gently lifted the baby and snuggled her comfortably in her arms. Pulling down the pink cotton blanket to expose Chalice's full face, she gasped. "This is not my son Nicky's baby!" In total hysteria she ran from the hospital room. Still groggy from the anesthetic, I thought she was shedding tears of joy!

Later I learned the truth—her outburst was shock and despondency motivated. She realized her son was not the father and perhaps thought he had been duped and coerced into a marriage of reparation!

Recovery from the C-section and the complications I suffered required a prolonged hospital stay which turned out to be a benefit. Aware of my young, not-quite-twenty age and inexperience, the nurses were helpful in teaching me some basic infant care skills.

When I was fully recuperated, my doctor came in to sign the papers for my release from the hospital. "Take good care of yourself and this child," he said, patting my hand. "Thanks to the miracles of modern medicine we were able to save you and successfully deliver your beautiful baby girl. If we had this same situation decades ago, we would have lost both you and the child. "Margaret," he continued, "I don't recommend any further pregnancies."

Realizing I was a complicated high-risk maternity patient, I listened to his words and thanked him for his role in obtaining my 'miracle.' However, in my heart I knew the truth—it was the will and mercy of God that preserved my life and gave Chalice hers!

Life was relatively peaceful for the first few months after Chalice's birth. I returned home and was attended to by my mother and grandmother. Both women were caring and a huge help in tending to my daughter's needs as a newborn, doting on us round the clock.

Regaining my strength, I had to face reality. I had a husband, Nicky, who I did not love and a situation to settle. Fearing John's threat to get full custody of the baby when she was born, I gave Chalice Nicky's name even though he was not the biological father.

In view of my restless, unsettled and less than ideal past, John did not need the expertise of a legal dream team to prove I was not equipped to care for the child in the manner in which he could with his affluent financial status, professional stability and solid family backing.

Soon after, Nicky and I had the marriage annulled. Despite our break-up and Nicky's eventual remarriage, he and his family continued to visit Chalice. They took her on outings and bought her clothes.

Chalice started to grow from an infant to a curious toddler soon inquiring about where she came from. I answered her question by telling her she was implanted by God, since I honestly believed, in part, it was true. Undoubtedly, Chalice was a gift from God, a gift that would open up a new and better life for us both.

I was pursuing the Catholic religion more seriously, though not yet actually studying to receive the sacrament of baptism. Still I prayed consistently, invoking the Lord to give me the strength to triumph over my demons and overcome the hurdles placed along my path.

Since I wanted no dealings with John despite his affluent status, I chose not to sue him for child support. Therefore, handling alone the financial aspects of my life at this stage was challenging. I needed more money than the car wash position paid and opted to follow the advice of a friend of mine, Kathy, who was dating the manager of a Chili's restaurant just opening in the area. "Margaret," she said, "come on over with us. We're all going to try to get jobs there. The tips are good and it will be fun."

I interviewed and was offered a waitress job. Kathy was taking care of the books and absolutely miserable, preferring to wait tables. Her boyfriend had mentioned the restaurant was seeking another full-time booker and she suggested me. "No, Kathy," he responded, "Margaret has neither experience nor formal training. I'm afraid she won't be able to handle it."

"But she's smart," Kathy interjected, "I know she can learn. I'll train her."

Although my formal education was obtained through various continuing education programs, I had no records or diploma to document my high school classes.

But believing in me, Kathy took me under her wing for two weeks, after which I was hired as a full-time bookkeeper for Chili's restaurant. Without a formal education it was not an easy task to find decent paying employment in the late 1980s work force. However, turning to my God, I knew beyond any doubt He would provide me with a means to support myself and my child and make certain that each part of the journey would prepare me for the next.

Certain that with the Lord's blessing I could do it all, I took on the bookkeeping challenge, intent on doing the absolute best job possible. I did all the books including the liquor counts, unaware that 'tomorrow' I would put to good use all that I was learning 'today!'

Thankfully, my Aunt Andy, grandmother Donna's daughter took care of Chalice while I worked. A warm, caring woman, I was blessed to have her in my life, knowing full well it was all a result of the goodness of God.

I recognized the value of gratitude and learned to appreciate my blessings, even if I still had obstacles and surprise curve balls to deal with from time to time.

John found out where I was working and started coming to the restaurant during the hours I was 'waitressing.' Incessantly badgered by family and friends for not forcing him to contribute financially, I refused, wanting nothing from him except total absence from my life and Chalice's.

Based on his copious income and net worth, the attorney told me I would be entitled to a very substantial sum of money from John every month in child support. I almost gagged—but it didn't tempt me. It was not about money—it was about getting this hateful stalker as far away as possible.

After my Juvenile Hall, South Wood, abusive home life, and foster care experiences, I felt like shattered glass. All I wanted was a reprieve from the confusion and chaos—I wanted a bit of peace of mind and serenity.

One day John presented himself at Chili's. "Margaret," he said arrogantly, "I'm going to marry a wonderful woman with whom I am in love. This is the real thing—not what we had."

I felt a weight lift from my chest—maybe I was finally seeing the last of John.

"Margaret," he continued straight-faced, "when Chalice grows up and asks about her father, just tell her I'm dead!"

Curt, irritable and intolerant he appeared to be a man filled with ethical challenges.

I knew I had the confirmation I had made the right decision—once again God had directed me in the right direction. His grace delivered me.

Chapter 9

God Gathered My Tears and Poured Them Down the Drain

"Deep waters cannot quench love, nor floods sweep it away. Were one to offer all he owns to purchase love, he would be roundly mocked."
—Canticle of Canticles 8:7

Prayer helped me build and fortify a strong relationship with God. My dialogues with Him became more frequent and intense, serving as an arm against human frailties, empowering me to defeat Satan's temptations. But more importantly, the time I spent in communion with the Lord taught me how to speak His 'language,' understand His messages and follow to the best of my ability, the path He had set before me.

I addressed my Creator often, and when I did I found a deep inner peace invade my hollowness and relinquish my fury. The anguish, anxieties and distressing uncertainty weighing heavily in my heart, seemed to lift and float away. When alone in my room, I drew the curtain on life's failings and focused on earning God's approval.

The quiet time was my sanctuary—my place of light and inspiration—my hope. It seemed as if in times of hardship, during the emotional torrents and uncontrollable tempests of my bleakest moments, God would pull away the massive black clouds, enticing the sun to beam its warming rays through the tiniest cracks in my blinds.

I learned not only how to accept God's will, but how to recognize and find gratitude in my heart for the blessings received. Discovering deliverance in prayer, I unburdened my soul. With a small child to support I needed a better-paying job. Still an unqualified, inexperienced member of the work force, I begged God for assistance. However, realizing I had to contribute to the employment process, I picked up the Classifieds, grabbed a pencil, and read through the offerings.

One ad caught my eye. It was an insert from a software company, advertising for a trainer. Recognizing I was somewhat of a long shot, and ignoring I had perhaps not even a slight chance, I completed a resume and sent it in.

Summoned for an interview, I discovered, at twenty-two, I was the youngest candidate applying for the position. Most of the applicants were in their forties with at least two decades of professional experience. It was unlikely I would even be seriously considered.

Returning home, I phoned my mother. "I doubt I will be called back," I told her. "I can't compete with the other individuals who have years of work experience."

"Margaret," she responded, "maybe you better look elsewhere. You're getting hired for the job is a long shot."

That evening, I received a call informing me the position was open if I was still interested. Upon accepting, I was given an official job description and learned I would be expected to cover many road miles every day. Somewhat apprehensive about the traveling part, I wondered if my old car would withstand that much driving.

"Mom, I was hired," I said, "but I don't know if my car will hold out."

"You actually got the job" she blurted. "Well, I'll help you with some financing for a new car."

Unable to purchase my own vehicle, my mother made it easy for me to get a new Hyundai. Her sudden willingness to participate in my life was surprising. Apparently, she was concerned about my ability to support myself and Chalice, and as a business analyst she also traveled extensively. Consequently, I believe she felt more at peace knowing I had a good job and the possibility of caring for my own little family.

Once hired, I completed a few months of training before being sent out on the road. Asking God to accompany me on this leg of the journey, I forged ahead, well-intentioned to do the best job possible.

Even though my yearly income was just $24,000, I was successful and enjoyed the experience. Thanks to the goodness of God, I was able to get my foot in the door and prove my worth.

Several months later, struggling to tote a tall stack of computer manuals to my car, I noticed another vehicle cross my path en route to picking up one of the employees who was waiting near the entry. In the driver's seat sat a woman and directly behind her, I saw the outline of what appeared to be a gentleman. With the manuals practically blocking my vision, it was difficult to discern further.

Unbeknown to me, the young man had inquired about the identity of the *petite* girl carrying a load of books taller than she! A couple of days later when I returned from a business trip I was informed I had received several messages. However, since I did not recognize the name, I had no idea who was leaving me the messages. Traveling extensively, I often handed my business card to numerous individuals. Perhaps the author of the messages was even a parking attendant. After all, I was young and single, and therefore available prey.

The messages continued to flutter in, and I persisted in ignoring them. My job kept me busy and on the go with little if any time to romanticize about a mysterious gentleman for whom I had neither a face nor an interest in my mind.

The following weekend I received a call from one of my colleagues, Virginia, although we were not particularly friendly. "Margaret," she said, "I'd like to invite you to my home for dinner. My roommate's brother just arrived here after graduating from the Naval Academy and he really doesn't have any friends or know anyone. Since you are the same age, I thought it might be fun if you met. You could introduce him around to other young people."

"Sure," I said, "no problem. I'd love to come."

I had absolutely no idea God was repositioning me—I was a pawn in my Creator's Hand, being moved along the chessboard of life. Neither did I recall the school-girl wish I made when I met Dawn's husband, Larry—but God remembered!

When I arrived at Virginia's house, I realized I had been set up on a blind date with her roommate Jean's brother, the gentleman who had spotted me lugging the tower of manuals in my arms. I also discovered he was the man behind the incessant telephone messages I had so discourteously ignored.

Jean's brother, Anthony, at six foot two was a striking gentleman. Athletic and handsome, he epitomized the attractive attributes of his Sicilian heritage. Inheriting the dark hair and creamy olive complexion of his Italian parents, he struck quite an imposing image. A pair of expressive green eyes exposed the transparency of his brilliant mind and captivating soul.

However, it was not Anthony's exceptional good looks that attracted me. Still not seriously interested in men, it was his solid character that caught my attention—Anthony was not dysfunctional!

Instead, as a graduate of Annapolis, he was the embodiment of the school's mission statement—*"To develop midshipmen morally, mentally and physically, and to imbue them with the highest ideas of duty, honor and loyalty."* This is precisely what Anthony represented to me—integrity, perseverance, determination and strength and this is why he captured my heart. He was reared in a close-knit, loving family who never skimped on love, affection and attention. Basically, he had the family and life I wished for in my fantasies.

Anthony had been assigned to the USS Tripoli, as a naval officer. Oddly, Dawn's husband Larry, the man I always considered an ideal mate, had also worked on the USS Tripoli, holding the same Ensign, junior rank of commissioned officer, as Anthony. Furthermore, the men shared an amazing physical resemblance.

Anthony and I met on April 16, 1990 and bonded immediately, becoming inseparable whenever he was on dry land. Although our courtship was lengthy, during the six years in which we dated, he was away often nine months at a time in areas that were not necessarily safe. The Persian Gulf War had left the military in perilous positions. Consequently, our separations were not without anxiety and concern.

Early one morning at five o'clock, my mother had heard that the USS Tripoli was seriously damaged. She phoned to speak with Uncle George who after the divorce and resulting loss of his home to my Mom, came back to live with me. He felt he could be of help since I now had a daughter to tend to and a rather time-consuming job.

"George," she said, "I don't want to upset Margaret needlessly, but you have to wake her up. Anthony's ship has been hit! No one knows how many were hurt or the nature of the injuries. Get Margaret on the phone."

Immediately, Uncle George ran to my room. "Margaret," he said, shaking me. "Margaret, your mother is on the phone—she wants to speak to you." He lifted the receiver and placed it over my ear.

"Margaret," my mother shouted, "are you there? Margaret, Anthony's ship has been hit! They don't know how badly or how serious the injuries to the crew may be."

I didn't wait to hear more. I threw the phone across the room and covered my ears with my trembling hands. Seconds later, hit with the reality of the situation and the gravity of the potential consequences, I shouted hysterically, "Please, God, keep Anthony safe. Don't let anything bad happen to him. Let him come back home safely."

Once Uncle George regained his composure from my sudden, unexpected violent outburst, he walked over, picked up the phone and put in back on my nightstand. "Be calm," he said almost hoarsely, "there are no official reports about fatalities or serious injuries. We really don't know anything, but your mother wants you to turn on the news."

Regaining a bit of my composure I jumped out of bed, snatched the phone and called Anthony's sister. "Jean," I screeched into the phone, "did you hear? Anthony's ship has been hit. We don't know if he's OK or not!"

"Come on over," she said sighing, "we'll listen to the news together." I dressed myself, praying. Repeating God's name, I went over to Jean's—never pausing even for a second to implore the help and mercy of God. *He* could not disappoint me—*He* had to deliver Anthony to me. He was an omnipotent God—there was nothing He couldn't do!

We sat glued to the TV for endless periods of time, desperate for the one reassuring word we so desperately wanted to hear. Since I was not Anthony's wife, I was not eligible to be contacted with any news or updates regarding his whereabouts or safety. Consequently, I was totally dependent on his mother, which was somewhat uncomfortable considering she did not have a fondness for me. Perhaps I did not fit the stereotype woman they had in mind for their Ensign son.

Unfortunately, Anthony's mother did not give me any updates regarding her son's situation and I had to wait, either until there was an official communication or one of his family members would let me know the status of the USS Tripoli.

Anthony's mother had set up her own little *santuario*, a shrine where she placed candles in front of the treasured statue of her favorite saint, *San Antonio*. On her knees amid the burnt wax fragrance of blazing candles, she chanted in her native tongue, imploring *San Antonio* for her son's safe return.

Afterwards, distraught and inconsolable *Signora* Iuculano took to the couch, consuming very little food and water for days, unduly worrying her husband and children.

With Anthony's mother becoming the new focus of concern for the family, I was pushed farther into the background. However, although I was considered the 'outcast,' I was constantly praying for the love of my life.

Years earlier when I had met Dawn's husband Larry, I had wished for a man just like him. With Anthony, my wish was granted. I had been sent "my very own Larry." Now, fearing the worst, I hoped God would come through again and deliver him home safely.

Unable to eat or sleep, I spent my evenings in prayer and conversation with the Lord. I would periodically doze off, then awaken to the awful reality that left me in tears and shuddering in fright.

Finally during the pre-dawn early morning hours, exhausted and drained, I fell into a deep sleep. Blessing me with a dream, God brought Anthony to me. I saw his glistening green eyes and broad smile. I felt his strong, reassuring hands gently nudge my shoulders. His face was so close to mine as he leaned over.

"Margaret," he whispered, "I only have a minute. But you have to eat and go back to work. Anthony is going to be OK." He turned on his heels, and I noticed how crisp his naval uniform looked. It was as white as a cloud on the sunniest of days.

"Don't go," I cried, extending my hand to grab his arm.

"Margaret," he responded, "I'm so very sorry, but I cannot stay. I was just sent here to give you that message. I have to go, now." As my heart raced I noticed he continued walking away from me until he evaporated into the wall.

Convinced God had sent me a message not to worry, I awakened feeling refreshed and grateful. After breakfast, I dressed myself and went to work. Drawn from my state of 'waking death' I re-entered the world of the living.

Eventually, I learned the ship had been hit by a mine, tearing a twelve by twelve foot hole in its starboard side bow. A repair locker had also been hit, blowing out a huge part of the ship. Although there were no fatalities, after the actual rescue, it took three months to get the damages repaired. This prolonged his tour abroad.

When Anthony did phone, he spoke of the sharks and venomous sea snakes patrolling the Persian Gulf waters in which the USS Tripoli was stuck. Thankfully, I was unaware of the dangerous nature of these paddle-tail reptiles without gills that had to come up for air to breathe. I was just grateful he was alive and well.

Upon Anthony's return he settled in San Diego. We continued to see each other frequently, growing closer and more united. While Anthony pursued his naval career, I worked and took care of Chalice.

A couple years thereafter, he received word the navy was transferring him to Annapolis, Maryland to complete shore duty at the academy for one of the admirals.

Much as Anthony and I were in love and committed to each other, we were young and not quite certain about jumping into marriage. As a Roman Catholic he took the Sacrament of Matrimony seriously, unwilling and fearful to even consider divorce.

"Why don't you and Chalice come to Annapolis with me," he suggested. "We can use the time as a trial period to see how living together would work out for us." Realizing I would be spending more time with Anthony if I lived with him, I agreed, convinced it was a novel idea.

However, when Anthony informed his family about our latest relocation plans, as expected, *Signora* Iuculano received the news neither with a smile nor delight. Realizing the relationship was serious, she feared her *bambino ed ultimogenito*, baby and youngest child, born when she was in her late forties, had fallen into the grips of a 'less than naive' single woman with a child. Convinced her cherished son was heading into a bad situation, she demonstrated her disapproval openly, neither with subtlety nor discretion.

Una donna senza passato—a woman without a past was her dream for Anthony, and I certainly did not fit the profile. I had more obstinate '*Gordian knots*' to cut than most individuals twice my age. However, there was absolutely no way I would receive her blessing. In her eyes, *non ero degno di lui*—I was just not worthy of her son.

Of course little if any diplomacy was used to repudiate me. In a few demeaning words I was labeled *persona non grata*—which meant my presence in their home was unwelcome. I knew I would eventually be able to overcome even this hurdle with a lot of prayer. I felt reassured God would enlighten their souls and clear their visions, allowing them to see me for who I am. I knew it would not be an easy task—I had to have patience and perseverance, but most of all I had to have faith.

Sadly, announcing our new living arrangement only seemed to confirm their unfavorable, almost hostile opinion of me. Thankfully, Anthony neither took seriously nor was influenced by the 'family point of view' in my regard.

"When they get to know you better," he would say reassuringly, "they will change their minds. Just give them time. You have to understand, it's a cultural thing."

On the other hand, my mother absolutely adored Anthony and Uncle George, in total agreement, held him in high honor. "He's a good solid man, Margaret," he'd say. "Anthony will make you happy."

Well I thought, at least my dysfunctional family has given their blessing. Anthony's family would have to deal with their own *Sword of Damocles* and learn to understand and accept the fate I was dealt in my early years. Although I was no longer that angry, scared faithless person, she would always be responsible for who I am.

I was rebuilding my relationship with my mother and Uncle George. After the divorce he seemed to have mellowed. Intent on helping me out with Chalice, he was, I had to recognize, a different man.

Amazingly, both my parents seemed to be reaching out to me. Accepting this turn of events as a gift from God, I refrained from questioning their motives, fearful and unwilling to point a finger at guilt.

Life was by no means perfect. Financially disadvantaged, I could not help but feel agitated and frustrated I had a responsibility to take care of Chalice, and I didn't like having to depend on others.

I realized Anthony's suggestion to move to Annapolis together was the answer to my dilemma. It promised a certain security, both financially and emotionally, and best of all I would be independent from my own family.

The move from California to Maryland gave me a new hope and the renewed optimism that springs from change. Of course, Anthony's family did not relax their obstinate condemnation of me, but I continued to ask God to 'take over and resolve this hurdle.' The more they protested and criticized, the more convinced I was that God had hand picked Anthony for me. He stood up to his family, defending and protecting me from their slings and arrows.

It was apparent he loved me and despite *Signora* Iuculano's unrelenting crusade to eliminate me from her son's life, his commitment to me and Chalice deepened.

I was enthusiastic about seeking new employment. However, my job experiences in San Diego were insufficient to qualify me for most positions in Maryland. I did not have the education needed to catch the attention of a human resources director.

After six months of plowing through classifieds, faxing resumes and waiting for calls that seldom if ever arrived, I was a bit overwhelmed with the new set of challenges. One evening, agitated and nervous, I had a rather heated discussion with Anthony. He was irritated and lost his patience, and it seemed as if our relationship might be a bit too shipwrecked to rescue.

The shouting match became overly heated. Scared things would be said I cared neither to hear nor say, I ran up the steps two at a time. Like a wounded, terrified soldier fearing for her life, I couldn't get off the battlefront fast enough! Seeking refuge in the bathroom I lowered my head into my hands and sobbed, "God, where are you? I need your help desperately. Please intervene. My life seems so messed up. I don't have a job and Anthony and I are fighting. God, please help me."

A week later while walking through a career event at the grand opening of a new Nordstrom's in Annapolis, I stopped by the human resources table to inquire about any possibilities for employment.

Hired on the spot, I immediately recognized the intervention of the Lord. "Thank you, God," I whispered as I filled in the necessary paper work. The job was in cosmetic sales and I was excited, knowing Anthony would be proud of me and we would slip into a smoother, less confrontational lifestyle. I would feel calmer and more productive and he would feel less financial pressure.

God had glued my life together again! He wanted me to realize it was time to stop crying and move forward. Obedient, at least to God—I did.

Two years later, with the honorable completion of six years of service, Anthony's commitment with the navy expired. Recruited by Corning Incorporated, he was offered a position which required relocating to Corning, New York, a city on the Chemung River with a population under ten thousand. Apart from Corning Inc, the Corning Museum and the Rockwell Museum of Western Art, there was nothing else to excite me.

Besides this grim geographical profile to dull my smile, there was the fact that I was excelling in my job at Nordstrom's. I enjoyed the day to day contact with customers and was earning a pretty decent salary. Furthermore, I had been promoted to manager in the cosmetics department and was rather pleased with the way my career was progressing. Consequently, Anthony's less than thrilling news involving another move did not sit well with me—I just did not want to pack up and go. Moreover, I was intentioned to stand firm on my decision.

I was not his wife, and leaving a secure job for an unknown future disturbed me. After all having a child to support was a serious long-term obligation. I prayed for guidance and for the ability to resolve the quandary.

Anthony listened to my concerns with an open mind. "Margaret," he said, smiling but tense, "I agree with your reasoning. However, I want to accept the position at Corning, and I want us to be together. I think it's time— will you marry me?"

Thrilled to hear the man I love—my Divinely chosen mate propose marriage, I could not give my consent quick enough. "Yes, Anthony," I blurted, "I'll marry you and go to Corning!"

In the same breath but with dramatically diminished volume I said, "Thank you, God."

The following day Anthony, still in uniform, appeared in the jewelry department at Nordstrom's to custom design an engagement ring. A real head turner with his handsome face and unique 'accessories,' he easily charmed all my colleagues. They celebrated my joyous moment perhaps with a bit of envy in their hearts.

Since my 'husband to be' was busy and unavailable, when I received word the ring was ready, I picked it up and placed it in my handbag. As soon as I saw Anthony, even if he was behind the wheel driving, I snatched it from my bag, tore off the pretty wrapping, flipped open the box and slipped my finger into his ring. I was now officially spoken for! "It's beautiful," I said, dangling my finger in his face. I guess it was obvious I was delirious with joy. That evening I went to sleep with the words, 'Thank you, God' on my lips.

Soon after, Anthony and I packed up our belongings and departed for Corning, New York. Impulsive as always I strolled into a medical company that handled the software programs for thirty-four clinics. I inquired if any positions were currently available. Receiving an affirmative response, I applied for one.

That evening I discussed the day's events with my mother who had remarried and was employed as a software analyst. "You can't do that job, Margaret," she said. "That's beyond your capability. You don't have the training or knowledge."

Thankfully, by now I was immune to the negativity of others and learned to pay no heed to the criticisms I received. Instead, I accepted the job when I was hired on the spot, grateful to God for His vote of confidence in me. I knew this was His will and I knew once again, He was directing my life.

My salary was $40.000. Thrilled, I reacted as if I had been offered a million dollars! Professionally secure, Anthony and I planned to marry on April sixteenth, exactly six years after our 'blind date' meeting.

Since *Signora Iuculano* was not overly fond of me and somewhat reluctant to give her blessing, to avoid undue distress and argument, perhaps even insult and injury, we decided to elope.

Flying to Jamaica, Anthony and I synchronized our marriage and honeymoon. It was a beautiful sunny day. The sky was deep azure and cloudless. In harmony, like bride and groom, the sea was calm and iridescent, glistening under the bright rays, as if buckets of diamonds had been poured over the minute ripples.

Anthony was mesmerizing in his pearl white officer's dress uniform, and I had purchased an equally splendid white dress. On a pier, under God's watchful eye and with the sun and sea as our witnesses, Anthony and I promised to love, honor and respect each other until death would part us.

When the 'I dos' were said and the rings slipped on our fingers, the Catholic island priest announced in heavily accented English, "I now pronounce you husband and wife."

Filled with joy we celebrated our love and union on the exotic island before our return back to California to visit with Anthony's family and mine. Surprisingly, *Signora*

Iuculano planned a nice reception for us, and together with my mother, those closest to us were able to toast the start of our new life as Mr. and Mrs. Anthony Iuculano.

After the wedding celebrations we returned to Corning. Chalice was now in school and ready to begin religious instruction. Since I felt I had waited long enough to pursue my own spiritual education, I thought it would be opportune to study alongside her. Furthermore, in my heart I knew the time was right for me to officially embrace the Catholic faith.

I enrolled Chalice in CCD, the Confraternity of Christian Doctrine course and went with her. Upon completion, nine months later, we were ready to receive the Sacraments of Baptism, Holy Eucharist and Confirmation.

Finally on a cold, snowy day, I was ready to become cleansed of my sins and united with my God. Chalice and I prepared ourselves and went over to the church. Stepping inside, I felt a shiver run down my spine—"It's freezing in here," I whispered through chattering teeth.

The church was chilly and I wondered how Chalice and I would feel having icy water poured over our heads. My thought was interrupted when the priest came forward. I smiled, feeling guilty about my less than spiritual thoughts and extended my hand in greeting. "Margaret," he said, "we wanted to heat the water a bit but the Jacuzzi didn't work this morning. I'm awfully sorry. It might be a bit uncomfortable, especially for your little girl, but God will be looking down on you from above."

Hearing his kind apology and encouraging words warmed my heart, strengthening my desire to become a 'child' of God.

No longer feeling the numbness in my feet, I took Chalice's cold little hand and walked with her to the baptismal font. Anthony's family was in attendance and his Aunt Zina and Uncle Joe were our Godparents.

Although I had initially encountered a bit of difficulty learning, understanding and interpreting the different doctrines of the faith, primarily because I felt the sisters did not use simple vocabulary, I was inspired to complete the course and reach this beautiful moment.

Plus, I wanted to be baptized and would never think of disappointing God. After all, He was always there for me. Realizing He had turned my life around, I strongly felt I should now offer every moment of my thoughts and actions back to Him in gratitude. In fact, my sole objective was to demonstrate to my Creator that I was willing to fully participate in every aspect of faith by becoming a Roman Catholic.

Stepping forward to receive the special anointment of salvation and spray of holy water on my head, I felt a rising calm unlike any other I had previously experienced. The words of Jesus written in Chapter twenty-eight of the Gospel of Matthew came into my mind: *"Go, therefore and make disciples of all nations, baptizing them in the name of the Father and of the Son, and of the Holy Spirit."*

And as the priest baptized me drizzling water over my forehead, I repeated the words in silence. Now a new child of God, I was empowered, lifted from my earthly path and ousted from my worries and concerns. I felt a strong Divine Presence descend upon the church. It brought such warmth, excitement and joy.

God had witnessed my act of devotion and my commitment to honor and serve Him. In return, He granted me an abundance of graces and the power to overcome whatever I truly wanted.

I had the confirmation the Lord was guiding my life, and I felt energized to move forward and complete the purpose He designed for me.

After the festivities, I returned to work and learned the company was in financial trouble. In addition I discovered there were envious, unscrupulous individuals seated in the corporate office. Driving a brand new car, I was devastated to notice it had long scratches running across the front door on the driver's side. It was more than evident it had been spitefully keyed!

Apparently someone felt threatened by my presence in the company. I moved my vehicle to the secure parking which had guards in attendance. Still I was keyed. The environment had become decidedly nasty and unpleasant.

"God, I prayed, help me find a better job. Something is not right here." I received a lead about a new job opening at Corning where Anthony worked. Once again the family feedback was dire. "Margaret, this is out of your league. You cannot believe Corning will hire you at that salary without any degree. They only hire graduates of top notch universities."

They were right about one thing—I did not have a degree. But what they didn't know was that God was in command, not Corning. That evening I prayed to God for a better job.

Less than twenty-four hours later at seven AM the following morning, I received a call offering me the job at a higher entry pay than Anthony had initially received as an Annapolis graduate! Plus, I was hired without passing through the standard multi-interview process, a protocol Anthony and others had to follow.

Qualified or not, the point was Corning spotted something in me that led them to believe I had the potential to be trained to handle the job description. Even Anthony was shocked.

I was now in management and often my fast moving career path was questioned by my family. "How can this be—Margaret has no skills and no higher formal education—yet she gets all these promotions and good jobs?"

Everyone was looking for explanations—but no one thought about God! No one realized He was my strength, my knowledge, my courage and my drive to succeed!

Once again, I was productive and soon received a monetary raise from my boss, Richard Luden, also a Naval Academy graduate. As in the past, my colleagues who had been with the company for years were envious of my quick, steady climb up the corporate ladder. Soon, I was friendless and unhappy. My vivacious personality seemed somewhat suffocated.

Noticing my beaten spirit and often teary eyes, Richard summoned me. "Margaret," he said, "you have to learn how to accept constructive criticism and use it to become a better person. You have to realize you are in a management position and must deal with other people. I will help you because judging from what I know about your past, I don't think you have much experience in this area."

I was convinced Richard was a guardian angel sent by God who took me under his wing. An older gentleman, he was kind, attentive and interested in my professional life.

Setting aside a couple of hours from his super-busy work day, he created a specially designed career path plan for me which would encompass several months. His goal was to educate by sharing the wisdom and knowledge he had acquired along his own career journey.

I returned to my desk, feeling uplifted for the first time since I began the Corning job. Several weeks later, motivated by Richard's plan, I dove into my latest project, unaware I was part of a team implementing new software that although globally coveted, was not yet available. I was overwhelmed, but thanks to my guardian angel and my God, I was able to complete the project.

Even though my career was blossoming, I just couldn't get acclimated to Corning, New York. Despite my open, outgoing personality, I had not made any friends. At work the environment was somewhat hostile.

One evening after dinner while discussing our corporate day, I threw an unanticipated question at Anthony. "What would it take for us to leave Corning?" I asked.

He seemed startled. "Margaret," he replied, clearing his throat, "I'm happy at Corning. I don't have any immediate plans to leave the company."

"But," I persisted, "how can I get you to change your mind?"

He gazed at me in silence for a few seconds. "Well," he said, "for one thing you would have to find a job offering you more than double your current salary."

"OK," I blurted, "this means you will consider leaving if I find a position that would pay me at least $85,000!"

His eyes widened. His lips remained sealed. His hand lifted, settling snuggly under his chin. I knew my husband was deep in reflection.

"Anthony," I said, interrupting his thoughts, "you know that if you give me a goal I will focus on it until I achieve it."

"OK," he said, grinning, "if you find a job paying $85,000, we'll leave Corning."

That evening I put my resume on Monster.com, a strategy I had never before considered. I prayed long and hard before retiring asking God to 'rescue me from Corning' and let me continue along my professional climb.

The following day I was inundated with calls from recruiters. I spoke with numerous consulting firms, and seven days later I made my decision. I accepted a job offer paying $85,000! Perhaps I could have gotten a more lucrative deal—but hearing the magic 85,000, I jumped, realizing it was my ticket out of Corning, New York en route to my next destination.

At this point, even agnostics had to believe in the influence of God in my life. It was downright blatant!

Anthony kept his side of the deal. He resigned from Corning, and we relocated to Atlanta, Georgia, for a short period prior to settling in Tampa, Florida. Amazingly, before celebrating our first anniversary, we had purchased our first home, Chalice and I had entered the church, and I was offered a job at double my previous salary. Who could doubt the repeated intervention of God in my life?

"But Jesus said to him, If thou canst believe, all things are possible to him who believes."
—Mark 12:22

Lessons Learned

Chapter 10

Banquet of Forgiveness

"Bear with one another and forgive one another,
if anyone has a grievance against any other;
even as the Lord has forgiven you,
so also do you forgive."
—Colossians 3:13

Thanks to the efforts of my 'corporate' guardian angel, Richard Luden, I was set upon a new career path and actually felt more secure about my potential and capability to be successful at whatever job I was undertaking. I knew God was moving me along, and I also recognized that He was preparing me for my true professional calling—only the time was not yet right. Patience and a bit more experience were expected of me.

We moved to Tampa, Florida, after I had received my '$85,000 dream' job offer with Romac. The company, now known as K-Force was and is an international recruiting firm specializing in staffing organizations and business in the health science, financial and technology fields with qualified employees. I was hired to direct one of the new start-up divisions.

Reasonably apprehensive about not falling short of my goal to successfully conquer this challenge, I prayed as soon as I opened my eyes every morning, asking God to give me the wisdom, tenacity and sense of fair play I needed to get the job accomplished in the most productive manner possible.

"Please God," I whispered, sliding behind the wheel of my car, "guide my thoughts and actions today, and let me give the very best of myself to this work." I repeated my prayer until I arrived at the entrance of the building. Seeing the name K-Force in the parking area was the cue for the amen. It was time to conclude my morning dialogue with God. Energized, I was ready to confront the day, feeling secure I was fulfilling my Creator's wishes, doing exactly what I was meant to do.

I confronted each day eager to learn and move ahead along my professional path. Meanwhile, K-Force, intentioned on implementing its revenue stream, restructured their business model to include a merger and acquisition strategy to acquire additional companies.

Undoubtedly, this was untried territory—an entirely new frontier for me to cross. Again, prayer together with the help of my new boss, Joe, and mentor Rich Cocchiaro's training and counsel, I was able to apply my knowledge to learn this aspect of the business.

After carefully examining the new acquisition proposals, I concluded it was not opportune for K-Force to proceed with this approach. Expressing my opinion, I conveyed my reasoning regarding the different financial strategies and business plans involved and how I felt acquiring and merging these two companies, after considering the discrepancies, would not be opportune.

Unfortunately, my advice was not heeded. Romac opted in favor of taking on the new company which specialized in corporate technology training. I was placed at the head of this newly established division. Realizing it would be a challenge, I set my sights on succeeding.

Over the next few years thanks to achieving my professional goal, I was able to enjoy many luxuries most people only envision in their dreams. Romac/K-Force recognized my accomplishments and potential in the company. I was compensated not only for my work, but for my dedication to the Company.

Feeling proud of myself, I believed I had 'hit it big time.' What more could I possibly ask for? I was successful, and my earning drew me away from a life of deprivation.

Although I worked long and hard to get to where I had finally arrived, professionally, I was grateful to Romac/K-Force not only for the learning experience and the chance to prove myself, but for their monetary recognition of my success.

A few years later, beating all odds and contradicting my doctor's opinion and advice, I discovered I was pregnant again—this time with twins! Based on my medical history, my physician predicted another complicated pregnancy. I realized that dealing with a challenging career and a difficult pregnancy simultaneously would take every last morsel of my faith and strength.

However, after another thorny nine-month period and the loss of one of the babies after a partial miscarriage, my son Anthony junior was born on August 23, 2001. With his dark hair, round, sweet, innocent face, and glowing eyes he was just as adorable as his big sister Chalice.

Unfortunately, Anthony, junior had some worrisome difficulties taking his first breath, but the medical attention he received was a blessing. A blue baby, I was unable to cuddle him in my arms as I did with Chalice. However, gazing at his tiny body in the incubator, I gave thanks to God for the miracle of life. It was all worthwhile—the pain, hardship and tears.

There was much to celebrate. Anthony senior was the proud father of his little heir and *Signora* Iuculano thanked *San Antonio* for the special blessing. I, on the other hand was grateful because my mother-in-law had recognized my transformation and loved me as a daughter-in-law. Building a meaningful relationship, we had formed a close and solid bond.

Too busy to think of anything but the important purpose of my life, I no longer had time for the fears and anxieties that often arise even if unwelcome. Perhaps God had decided I had had enough. Gathering the final unpleasant insecurities, He removed them from my days. I had too much going for me to be sad or miserable, and I had a long intricate path ahead.

Although I recognized the precious gift God had given me in Anthony junior, I knew I was in for quite an interesting, if not challenging experience, juggling a high-powered career change and the needs and demands of a tiny infant. However, aware I was living in accordance with my Creator's *will,* I knew I could depend on Him for the strength to overcome any and all detours or hurdles that would eventually materialize. So, I took a deep breath and prayed.

I applied for maternity leave to recuperate from the birth of my son, gather my strength and tend to his needs during the first vital weeks of life. As always I was not in command. Apparently, God had other plans.

Soon after I returned from the hospital, I received a phone call from my boss. "Margaret," he said after inquiring about my health, "we need you here. You have to come back to work. Your division is not producing. We would like you to shut it down, give notice of termination to the employees and deal with the customers." I agreed to come in.

After much prayer and deliberations with God, followed by a careful evaluation of the situation, I realized the company was viable and potentially success oriented. I also discovered there was another option.

Pooling together our resources, Anthony and I devised a plan to purchase and rename the company and roll over the employees and customers. Not only was it feasible, it was what I was meant to do in this given moment in time.

The message was on the board—I had been prepared for this event. I was beginning to clearly discern the different facets of the Lord's plan for me. All the little steps and hurdles were to get me ready for this giant step. I felt in tune with God since I was moving along with His wishes.

The how, when and where elements of this company buy-out plan were still not plainly evident in my mind, but as a compensation my self-confidence rested with my faith in God. I strongly believed beyond any doubt reasonable or otherwise, that since He had led me here, He would be willing to un-clutter and light the path.

Within a short period of time, the financing required to set acquisition in motion started coming in. It was as if interested investors were sprouting like clusters of buds in early May.

God was working another miracle. Funds were accumulating and the company was moving towards fruition. Deals were being finalized and the earning was becoming noticeable.

Life at home was far from smooth, although I knew I could depend on God to bail me out whenever my challenges gathered more weight. At five weeks, my son Anthony suffered painful bouts of colic which prohibited him from sleeping more than two hours uninterrupted. Moreover, my SQ-stress quotient was soaring—new baby—new business; both required undivided attention, a ceaseless pervading spirit and a bottomless well of energy.

Forced to work fourteen-and fifteen-hour days brought me to the realization of the importance of education. At a striking disadvantage because of my dysfunctional childhood, I had to struggle more than most CEOs to successfully structure and run my company.

I was now beginning to visualize more clearly how the Lord's pan was unraveling. It became unmistakably evident as I backtracked and traced the different segments of my career path. I noticed that all my previous jobs in a sense served as a training period for my real professional purpose as an entrepreneur.

What I lacked in a formal education, God had given me in experience. Certainly it is not the route I would recommend as it was undoubtedly a more intricate, frustrating and thorny road to knowledge. However, despite the barricades to break through and the demons to stave off, my persistence, tenacity and determination all nourished by my faith in and dependence on God, made me a victor through all obstacles.

With a voracious appetite for learning, I hit the book stores, buying everything I could get my hands on relating to the business world. I read about corporate marketing and management and took it a step farther, enrolling in courses I felt would help me gain the know-how needed to not only revive a bankrupt company, but flip it into a successful enterprise.

Every challenge was a huge stumbling block, but every impediment I was able to encounter and surpass was another testimony to the influence of God in my life. Prayer brought *manna* into the wilderness of my life.

I now recognized the meaning behind my early professional trials and ordeals. I was being groomed for my role as corporate CEO of my own company. The journey was well plotted and distinctly mapped out—and now I had the map in my hand.

Previously, I had headed a division of K-Force, but managing a business when my own funds were involved was quite different from governing with investors' bank accounts. Anxious, frustrated and apprehensive, I was fighting a battle for survival, especially in the dawning stages of the business.

With the passage of ownership came a change in the company's identity. Renaming the business *Tech-Sherpas*,

I believed it was a clever marketing strategy, since *sherpas* are Nepalese Himalayan mountain guides. Therefore, applying the meaning to the main objective of the company—technological guidance, I felt it was more than befitting.

Although the name created a lot of contention, the controversy surrounding it served to place it in discussion and on the tongues of many people. Consequently, the company got noticed which is the primary objective of marketing.

When I first stepped in as owner and CEO, I had over thirty-five competitors to contend with. In addition, my timing was less than promising. The actual closing of the corporate buy-out coincided with the devastating 9/11 tragedy, bombarding me with almost immovable circumstances to defeat. The impact was beyond challenging.

Dividing my time among Anthony junior, my teenage daughter Chalice, and the Company left me barely a moment to breathe. My children were my primary focus, and God was the Master Architect, designing and presiding over the entire scenario.

Shortly thereafter, I discovered that thirty-three of my thirty-five competitors had filed for bankruptcy. Refusing to adhere to a doom and gloom domino effect, I prayed long and hard. "God—it's me, Margaret calling," I said, often during my waking intervals. "God, please, I need your help. All my competitors are folding. Help me stay afloat."

I had engaged my sister, Cindy, who made it known she was available to work for me, and trained her to assume the role as comptroller. Trustworthy and reliable, I recognized in my sister a valuable employee. Although not overtly religious, Cindy realized the potent influence of God in my life. "Margaret," she said one afternoon after reviewing the company books, "God is really watching over your shoulders. Somehow the money always comes in when it's time to make the payroll. It's incredible. We never miss once and we're never late!"

Thankful, I had to admit Cindy's observation was accurate. God kept the business moving even in a sloweddown economy still dealing with the overwhelming effects of 9/11. Times were difficult, and even the last two competitors who had survived until now, though barely making it, shut down.

Although the company was far from profitable, God rescued it repeatedly from falling under. He kept it alive and as the months and years passed, I began to fully recognize the real power behind the throne. I may have occupied the CEO chair, but it was God's business—as the Chief Executive Officer, He was running every aspect of the company through me.

As an entrepreneur, my goal was to create a profit-producing business and survive in the repressed economy of the times. However, as I became aware of the Divine Manipulation, my faith strengthened. In addition, I believed blessings given require acts of gratitude.

Despite the Lord's faithful intervention, my part in the company's success was a daily tussle. Undoubtedly, I was belted down and experiencing the ride of a lifetime. Often my 'vehicle' careened so close to the edge, only my steadfast faith kept me from tumbling out. Even invoking my Creator was exhausting. Fully conscious of His presence, I was certain I had to take the time to dialogue with Him. He wanted to hear from me all about my sorrows, fears and needs.

All through my conversations with God during which I meekly implored for assistance and guidance, surrendering my life to His Will, I recognized the lesson I was being taught. Humbled, time and time again, in the Divine Design, God transformed me step by step. Initially He cast me into the shade, removing all traces of joy and gratification from my life.

Although faultless, I was asked to submit to a spiritually nonexistent environment and live a calamitous life among predominately emotionally downtrodden individuals.

But God asked me to bear suffering and deprivation. Moreover, He paved the way for me to witness that very same agony and scarcity in others, to help me learn who I was and how far I had to go to become who I should be, to better resemble His likeness.

Every time I was humbled, I received the grace and strength to gather my forces and work towards raising myself up to where God wanted me to be. I had much to learn—and it wasn't all business. However, both my life and my company were in God's hands.

Chronically mistrusting of my fellow man, a side-effect of my disillusioned childhood, it was not an easy task for me to relate well to others. However, during my CCD classes with Chalice the nuns would often quote a passage from the Gospel of John 13:34: *"A new commandment I give you, that you love one another: that as I have loved you, you also will love one another."*

I repeated these beautiful words spoken to the twelve apostles, knowing in my heart this was expected of me. God wanted me to turn my back on my distrust and dislike of mankind and embrace humanity with love and forgiveness. Would my Creator's wishes be fulfilled, or would His expectations be met with blighted hope? Certainly unwilling to disappoint God, I promised I would try my best to spiritually energize my life.

Never a team player, I always concentrated on taking the leadership role in managing others. But with the passage of years, I began to take the time to get to know my employees as individuals, often becoming emotionally involved in their private lives.

I was moving into a new realm and treading on foreign soil. But despite the unfamiliarity, I liked the warm feeling spinning deep within my being—an energizing, yet comforting sensation that spread through my entire body whenever I extended an extra kindness to one of my staff members.

My Creator was working on me. No longer centered exclusively on my own financial needs and goal-driven intentions, I learned through my business dealings how to care for others. It was a major turning point in my life. I was not just a baptized Roman Catholic—I was living my life as a true Christian. It was an Act of God, a three hundred sixty degree change of course.

And participating unconditionally in my faith, I decided to join the C-12, a group of Christian entrepreneurs, CEOs and company presidents who share my firm believe that God directs also the business aspect of our lives. Committed to living according to God's wishes, the C-12 offers solidarity and the opportunity to grow and develop an interior life while running a productivity oriented business.

I agreed with their mission statement, ideals and strategies and felt I could prosper both spiritually and professionally by linking my business model to their concepts. Most of all I felt comfortable knowing God would fully bless my decision to gain membership in an organization that claims, *"How we conduct business defines much of who we are."*

C-12 'preaches' that the company belongs to God. We, the owners and CEOs are 'employed' by God to lead and direct business activity, always mindful of and respecting moral and ethical codes.

Joining the C-12 gave me the wonderful opportunity to meet Ed Phillips, the group leader. Thanks to Ed's efforts and attention, I was able to steadily move through a complicated process, holding on to my optimism.

Another 'guardian angel' sent by God, Ed encouraged me to step out of my comfort zone. His empowering words led me and the other members through challenging avenues. A charismatic motivator, he gave us the energy and a reason to move forward.

Observing like a doting parent, while we'd carefully tread new ground, Ed enjoyed charting our growth. Undoubtedly, it was a significant learning experience. God had put Ed on my path to guide me along the journey. However, I did not realize his powerful influence in my life until I had left the group.

During this amazing and enlightening period, I received proof of the existence of the law of reciprocity. All that I did of questionable integrity returned to haunt me. I paid for trampling on the trust Jim and Nancy demonstrated in me, when I behaved dishonestly at the *California Yogurt Company*. Now, God wanted me to learn the painful impact of my evil deed.

Destined to live that same sin—this time not as the sinner, but as the sinned against, I was in the Creator's role ready to experience the crushing repercussion of wrong-doing.

I had a wonderful general manager, Ray, a man of honesty and reliability who I loved and regarded as a brother. He was accepted as part of our family, and often Anthony and I invited him to share holidays around our table.

When other employees came to me, "Margaret," they would say, "we don't think Ray is a good general manager for the company," I'd always brush off their considerations as either rash judgments or verdicts based on corporate jealousy. After all, he was the privileged manager. And I didn't want to believe anything negative about Ray. My husband and I befriended him and we expected the same in return.

However, Ray was stealing from the company. One day I discovered I had been blocked from my own server and unable to access all the e-mails, corporate documents and files. Questioning the why behind this sudden unexpected 'lock out,' I found out that Ray was behind the shut down. Apparently, he didn't want me to read his correspondences. This deduction triggered a red flag. I had to dig deeper to uncover the motive.

I engaged a security consultant from my former employer, K-Force, who was currently working elsewhere.

He unblocked the server allowing me to access Ray's hard drive where I was able to bring his plan to light.

I discovered that in the secrecy of his office, Ray had back door keys with which he created code names to enter into our server from the outside, using various aliases.

Reading his e-mails left me in shock. My seemingly loyal and trusted friend and general manager was involved in a big scale deception, at my expense. He was stealing from the company and refusing to pass incoming contracts through the company. Instead, Ray was taking on the assignments as a private consultant.

Literally bolted out of the blue in the light of such flagrant evidence, I was beyond disillusioned. Offended, shocked and disappointed, I feared for the future of the company. Ray was the moving force, and I wondered if I could survive without him at the helm.

Of course I called on God, realizing how deeply I was hurting. Apart from the Golden Rule—*"Do unto others as you want done unto you,"* I recognized I was put into a position albeit years later, to live all the pain and sadness I had inflicted on Jim and Nancy when I stole money from them.

God was teaching a lesson in retributive justice. It was the Old Testament *lex talonis,* law of retaliation.

"...If the injury ensues, you shall give life for life,
eye for eye, tooth for tooth, hand for hand..."
—Exodus 21:23

I had unlawfully taken from another without conscience, and now another had improperly taken from me. Years back when I had committed the evil deed, thoughtless and ruthless, I had no idea how much hurt I had caused. That day I learned.

Surprisingly, God gave me the gift of forgiveness. It was almost instinctive and immediate. Without malice, ill-will or hatred for Ray, I accepted his misbehavior as a human failing. I searched in my heart, finding the clemency God had placed there. It was about forgiveness... *"Father forgive them, for they do not know what they are doing."*

Although I had no choice but to terminate Ray's employment with the company, I took the time to explain my decision. "Ray," I said after summoning him to my office, "considering the nature of our relationship, I don't understand why you did not come to me if you had a problem."

"Margaret," he whispered, avoiding my gaze, "I'm terribly sorry. I feel just awful and I understand your decision to fire me."

God had poured forgiveness into my heart. As a result I looked upon Ray through my Creator's eyes. He had sinned just like all of us. But if God could forgive, so could I! It was all part of the Divine Plan.

My spiritual growth was widening. I had re-established a relationship with Cindy after years of conflict and serious disaccord. We had been separated when she married. However, after a trying period followed by her crushing divorce, I invited her to Florida with the intention of alleviating some of her hardships by providing her with the possibility to have a better life.

As I helped Cindy gain the business skills needed to satisfy the requirements to assume a position in the

Company, we learned how to relate as sisters. In time we moved from our old Cain and Able rivalry into a relationship in which she became my most ardent supporter. Loyal and endearing, she stood by me like a Swiss Guard in the Pope's company.

Recognizing once again the healing power of God in my life, I prayed for the same gift of reconciliation to seed forgiveness and acceptance in my heart towards my mom and Uncle George.

During the past few years I had matured both professionally and spiritually. My hard work and diligence extended beyond my goal to build a successful, profitable company. I was also focused and committed to working on myself. A vital part of my strategy was to rebuild all the fragmented relationships with my family; bonds that had been shattered and seriously damaged during my tormented childhood.

A ravenous reader, I sought books to educate myself. However, not limiting my subject matter to business, I went for every self-help, personal improvement, and spirituality enhancing title on the market. Devouring the written pages with an almost insatiable appetite for knowledge, I applied what I absorbed to my life and situation.

Returning from work one evening, Anthony had to climb over a pile of books to get to where I sat. "I feel like I'm living in Barnes and Noble," he said, chuckling. "We must have thousands of books!"

He was right—there were books in every room—kitchen, hallways and bathrooms included. Every night when I slipped into bed, I had to push the books to one side in order to make space for myself. I took from each book something of value and applied it to the different facets of my life.

The Christian books taught me to love and emulate Christ. I learned how to regard my fellow human beings with patience, tolerance and love—the very same beings I always disliked, mistrusted and held at a distance.

But, perhaps the remarkable and imposing life-altering lesson I learned was how to let go of unrequited forgiveness. If I could be forgiven and forgive others, why couldn't I forgive myself?

Implanted with God's wisdom, I became familiar with self-reconciliation. I was able to absolve myself of the acknowledged wrongdoings that hurt others. But perhaps more importantly, I was able to move away from bearing malice towards myself and no longer harbored unchristian thoughts.

Surprising me one day, while I sat with my head rotating from one book to another like the pendulum of a clock, Anthony walked over. "Margaret, why don't you just read the Bible?" he asked. "For sure, you will find the answers and guidance you are searching for more easily than by buying and plowing through hundreds of books. You're reading everything in print but the Bible!"

I paused, put down my books and reflected a moment. "God," I asked softly, "are you speaking to me through Anthony?" Was I being sent a message?

Realizing my Creator often addressed me using emissaries, I began to pay more attention to the people who surrounded me. Listening to their comments and or criticisms, I no longer took offense or reacted with aggression to less than kind words. Instead, I looked for messages and words that would help me improve not only who I was, but how I personally perceived and treated myself.

Taking Anthony's advice to heart, I purchased a Bible. However, as I began reading I discovered the Sacred Book was written in a much more grandiose style with words and phrases that were rather complicated to grasp. Consequently, I had trouble understanding some of the passages. Although I felt a definite complicity with God, it often seemed as if I was reading His words in a foreign language and struggling to absorb the meanings.

A tenacious, solution oriented person, I returned to the bookstore and found a teaching Bible complete with original text and simple, clear explanations in plain English on the bottom. "Thank you, God," I said, as the cashier rang up the sale. I was so excited I could hardly wait to get home and devour it page by page.

My determination and persistence were commendable. If not exactly God-like, they were certainly saintly. I was unyielding in my quest for spiritual knowledge. I wanted to know my God, and I wanted to know everything about Him. I was relentless.

When I arrived home I quickly unwrapped the Bible and flipped though the pages, briefly scanning the back page comments. There was a sentence that caught my eye immediately. It was a bit of advice on "how to read the Bible in one year."

Excited, I mentioned it to Anthony. "This is what I will do," I said, "I'll get up earlier in the mornings and dedicate forty-five minutes to reading the Bible." And that's precisely what I did sticking to my schedule as best

I could. At the end of the year, I determined I was running behind by just thirty days—not bad for a wife, mother of two, and successful entrepreneur.

Although I still encountered challenging passages and difficulties with the not exactly popular bestseller writing style, I was mesmerized by the effect the Bible had on my life. I was drawn to it like bees to honey—for nourishment and for survival. Realizing the answers to my uncertainties and the remedy for my inner turbulence were contained within those pages, I prayed incessantly to God for help in understanding what He wanted me to learn.

The New Testament fascinated me. It was all about the life of Jesus Christ, in an empowering and educative manner. The parables were inspiring and imparted life-altering messages I could apply personally, although it took more than the first reading for me to 'get it.' However, as I pursued understanding,frustrating as it sometimes was, I unexpectedly noticed a special feeling of peace descend upon me like tongues of fire on the apostles.

Mysteriously, my anger and resentment, along with the all consuming demons that tried to chisel away at my being, disappeared one by one into nothingness. It was as if they were sucked right out of my spirit, by the hallowed breath of the Holy Spirit.

Suddenly there was an unfamiliar, but soothing quiet within. The churning stopped. The turmoil was silenced. The fear was subsiding. Freed from a demonic power, I was snatched away from Satan. This conniving demon masquerades his wicked sneers and evil tentacles behind many confusing disguises. Through those with feeble faith and drowsy morals he tries to seed chaos and adversity with his miserable presence. Always in conflict with the Lord, he meets his nemesis in a believer armed with the name of God.

"*And lead us not into temptation but deliver us from evil...*" I prayed as God banned Satan from my life turning my chaos into serenity—warming and filling the cold hollowness within.

I was a different person, renewed. I stepped from the darkness of my self into the enlightened radiance of a child of God, loving and pardoning my neighbor as myself. My family and the employees who surrounded me noticed the transformation—"Margaret, you seem so at peace with yourself and the world," they told me repeatedly. "You are no longer aggressive or condescending, even when things don't run smoothly. It's amazing!"

I walked around actually seeing the 'likeness of God' in my fellow human beings.

"*Forgive us our trespasses as we forgive those who trespass against us.*" Forgiving my mother and Uncle George was perhaps one of the greatest manifestations of my spiritual conversion. I learned total acceptance. They were who they were, but more importantly I recognized their frailties as part of the human condition.

I phoned them weekly, no longer motivated by obligation, but by a love for who they represented in my life. And surprisingly, although I did not receive an apology from Uncle George for all the wrongdoings committed against me, in a conversation one day, he did it his way. "Margaret," he said, "I wish I could do things over again. This time I would be a different father to you." Recognizing remorse, and witnessing how lovingly he treated his first grandchild, Chalice, I accepted even his terrible deeds, actually believing he may have behaved in a manner in which he thought best.

Although my mother and I did not have the relationship I had always wished for since childhood, God gave me the strength to understand and accept her for who she was and is. I try to the best of my ability, to keep our relationship intact and moving in the right direction, always praying and hoping that one day the past will no longer hinder or haunt how we feel about and relate to each other.

As time passed, my relationship with *Signora* Iuculano strengthened, becoming increasingly more agreeable. My bond with God deepened during the challenging five years in which I literally struggled, day and night to rehab who I was, in order to be praiseworthy to call myself a child of God.

As my journey for the truth brought me closer to achieving the inner harmony needed to become more in tune with my spirituality, my mother-in-law looked at me differently, actually seeing who I had become instead of who I was. Undoubtedly, I had become a different person.

I no longer took unkind words or deeds as a personal offense, but recognized we are all creatures of imperfection. Hatred and rancor were no longer seated in my heart. I realized that everyone was placed along my path for a reason.

My husband Anthony was a gift from God. Viewing him from a different perspective, I was always willing to accept him for who he was, fully conscious of his love and good intentions in my regard.

"Read the Bible," I responded, when people questioned me about my newfound peace. "Let God into your life." I truly believe anyone who is open to the power of God will experience the same radiance and rush of serenity. They will no longer walk in darkness. It was promised.

> *"I am the light of the world. He who*
> *follows me does not walk in darkness,*
> *but will have the light of life."*
> —John 8:12

Epilogue

My God Box

"You shall love the Lord, your God, with all your heart, with all your soul, and with all your mind. This is the greatest and the first commandment. The second is like it: You shall love your neighbor as yourself."
—Matthew 22:37-39

With the passing of time my faith grew and deepened. I lived each day with spiritual aplomb, gaining closeness and accessibility to God. Refusing to be badgered by the haunting specter of my past, I went forward renewed.

My prayer list was an endless series of dialogues with God which served to reinforce my relationship as every wish granted was the acknowledgment to the love and mercy of my Creator.

God was a constant in my life. He inspired my waking thoughts and sent me off in the evenings with a sense of peace and serenity. In response, I consulted Him daily. Prayer became my weapon to fight off the evils seeding doubt and uncertainty in my life. I unburdened my heart and offered my life to God. It was my salvation.

One afternoon while shopping, I stumbled upon an attention-grabbing, brown mahogany box. Inscribed in bold gold letters across the lid were the words, *My God Box*. Intrigued, I picked it up to get a better look. Lifting the top I noted a striking image of white clouds, beneath which were the empowering words: "*When your head starts to worry and your mind just can't rest, put your thoughts down on paper and let God do the rest.*"

Unable to curb my enthusiasm I blurted, "This is exactly what I need." What a novel idea and how very appropriate. I had prayer lists and scraps of paper with my scribbled thoughts tightly stuffed between the pages of my Bible and other personal items.

Sometimes I could hardly keep track of all my 'spiritual correspondences.' But this God Box was an ingenious idea. It would permit me to place all my wishes and 'transcripts' of my conversations with God in a special box.

Not only did I buy it on the spot, I took several and offered them as gifts to all those I felt would put them to good use. Now, I was spiritually organized. Whenever I addressed God through a handwritten wish or prayer, I slipped it into the box.

Every month or so I opened my God Box, rummaged through my prayer lists, and it was always awe-inspiring to bear testimony to my requests and wishes answered. Perhaps the most remarkable angle was the actual manner in which my intentions were fulfilled—in a more grandiose way than I ever possibly could have hoped for or imagined. Although at the time I may have been swimming in a dark channel regarding my own well-being, this was verification of the Lord's keeping my best interest at heart. Sometimes, disillusioned, we feel as if God has abandoned us or has opted to ignore our needs, however many times we fail to realize that what we ask for may not be always the most opportune appeal for our welfare.

What remains in my God Box are active requests awaiting a response. Usually the wishes and prayers I address to the Lord on behalf of others have a quicker response. But I confront each day with faith-fueled patience, recognizing the process is quite sacred and monitored exclusively by God.

About once a month I browse through the prayer intentions I slip in from time to time and pull out all those that have been resolved. What usually linger are my personal requests awaiting Divine attention.

Although I'm extremely happy to witness favors granted to others for whom I have implored, I am tenacious in praying for my own needs. God answers, sometimes after giving me a lesson in patience and persistence, and many times His resolution to an issue or dilemma differs from mine.

Throughout the years I have come to an understanding concerning God's wisdom and foresight. Realizing they far surpass mine, I have learned to trust His judgment and accept His solutions.

Through my years of suffering I have reached a greater appreciation for happiness and the blessings I have received. If fully embraced as part of God's plan, torments and afflictions are humbling and strengthening. The Holy Spirit used suffering as a vehicle to prepare my heart to receive God. Journeying to my own *Calvary*, I was saved from the hatred and anger that were consuming my heart. My eyes were opened to the majesty of my Creator. Implanted with the seeds of faith, I learned acceptance and forgiveness.

According to Mother Angelica at Eternal Word Television Network, it's an insult to God when you think your sins are greater than God's mercy. Therefore, to abstain from offending the Lord, I beg for forgiveness, then forgive others as I am forgiven.

Today, after running successful businesses, I have liquidated my companies and am empowered to step out of the entrepreneurial box and embark on a new journey. Feeling a strong calling to my mission to help abandoned, abused and un-adoptable children destined to grow up in foster care or state run systems, I am committed to making a difference. God and this book, *My God Box* will be my supporters and the means to obtaining my goal.

> *"Let the little children come to me, and do not*
> *hinder them for of such is the kingdom of God."*
> —Mark 10:14

Life spins, interrupting or halting its course for no one. Often I find myself trapped in surviving the day to day moments of a reality that prohibits me from stepping back and taking a look at what is happening around me. In the evening when my head touches the pillow, my thoughts turn to my abundant blessing and to those deprived children with whom I share a common experience. Just before my expressions of gratitude and my final prayers, one burning question churns in my mind: what have I done today for someone in need?

As I began the process of writing this book I felt a sense of calm and inner peace descend upon me. I realized I was using God's will to both motivate and empower me. He expected me to set down my suffering and heartaches to unhinge and enlighten the weak, the doubters, the desperate and the faith challenged to the power and existence of God.

I hope that many individuals living in the shadows will be inspired by *My God Box* to step into the radiance and either begin to build or solidify an existing relationship with God. It will bring a very special tranquility and instill a new perspective regarding the significance of life.

The future with its countless unknowns and uncertainties no longer scares or worries me. Focusing on each day, I commit to trying my utmost to do my best. Realizing that even my best is not always good enough for those around me, I think more compassionately about my parents whose best was just not good enough for me as a child.

Promising to always give the greatest of myself, I do realize my objectives and actions may not always culminate in the results I planned or desired. However, with an unwavering faith in God, resolutions to dilemmas and solutions to problems will unravel in the most favorable way possible.

Today, I accept suffering as part of the human condition—I suffer in serenity, knowing I have My God Box into which I place troubles and prayers for myself and for others.

Although faith guides my life, my days and evenings are certainly not without challenges. Disappointed? Absolutely not! Why? Because as I continue along my journey, I amass more knowledge, gain incredible strength and bond more deeply with God every time I overcome an obstacle.

My God Box sometimes runs over with requests, and as each one is answered in the way in which the Lord sees fit, I give thanks for the new and improved person I am becoming as a result of my continued trials. And in return I want to change the lives of abandoned, abused children. More importantly, I want to encourage them to understand that they can achieve their goals, realize their dreams and redirect their lives with just a mustard seed of faith. Through the power and presence of God in their lives, they shall be enlightened and empowered as I was.

"All power in heaven and on earth has been given to me. Go, therefore and make disciples of all nations, baptizing them in the name of the Father, and of the Son and of the Holy Spirit, teaching them to observe all that I have commanded you; and behold I am with you all days, even unto the consummation of the world."
—Matthew 28:18-20